Managing Resource Sharing in the Electronic Age

AMS Studies in Library and Information Science

MARY E. JACKSON, SERIES EDITOR

ISSN 1040-5631

Other titles in this series:

1. Mary E. Jackson, ed., Research Access through New Technology.

Managing Resource Sharing in the Electronic Age

Edited by
Amy Chang and Mary E. Jackson

AMS PRESS
New York

Library of Congress Cataloging-in-Publication Date

Managing resource sharing in the electronic age / edited by
    Amy Chang and Mary E. Jackson.
      p. cm. - - (AMS studies in library and information science; 4)
    Includes bibliographical references and index.
    ISBN 0-404-64004-4 (alk. paper)
    1. Interlibrary loans - - United States. 2. Document delivery -
-United States. I. Chang, Amy, II. Jackson, Mary E.
III. Series: AMS studies in library and information science : no. 4.
Z713.5.U6M36 1996   96-135
025.6'2--dc20   CIP

All AMS Books are printed on acid-free paper that meets the guidelines for performance and durability of the Committee on Production Guidelines for Book
Longevity of the Council on Library Resources.

AMS Press, Inc.
56 East 13th Street
New York, N.Y. 10003

MANUFACTURED IN THE UNITED STATES OF AMERICA

MANAGING RESOURCE SHARING IN THE ELECTRONIC AGE

CONTENTS

Foreword .... *Amy Chang*

I. RESOURCE SHARING : CORE COMPETENCIES

Chapter 1 .... Page 1
The Competitive Advantage Of Librarians: Core Competencies for
Document Delivery .... *Curtis L. Kendrick*
Introduction
Document Distribution Chain
Three Perspectives on Document Delivery
Critical Success factors for Document Delivery
Core Competencies for Document Delivery
From Mass Marketing to Relationship Marketing
Conclusion

Chapter 2 .... Page 13
From Paper Forms to Electronic Transmission: The Evolution of
Interlibrary Loan Electronic Technologies .... *Yem Siu Fong*
Introduction
Historical Overview
OCLC
ILL Management
Model Projects
Convergent Technologies
Implications of Technology
Conclusion

II. DOCUMENT DELIVERY IN THE 1990S

Chapter 3 .... Page 25
Document Delivery In The 1990s: An Overview .... *Lee Anne George*
Introduction
Document Delivery
Current State of Document Delivery
Document Suppliers
What Does the Future Hold?
Conclusion

Chapter 4... **Page 32**
    Ordering, Delivery And Turnaround: How Do Document
    Suppliers Maintain Their Markets? .... *Mary A. Hollerich*
        Marketing 101
        Document Suppliers
        Ordering Options
        Delivery Options
        Turnaround Time
        Conclusions

Chapter 5... **Page 43**
    Document Delivery: The Confusion of It All .... *Rosann Bazirjian*
                                                      and Pamela W. McLaughlin
            Introduction
            Definition of Document Delivery
            Proliferation of Available Services
            Evaluative Criteria
            Proliferation of Delivery Methods
            Conclusion

III. MANAGING INTERLIBRARY LOAN

Chapter 6... **Page 52**
    Total Quality Management for Interlibrary Loan and
    Document Delivery .... *Amy Chang*
            Introduction
            Challenges and issues for ILL/DDS
            TQM dimensions for ILL/DDS
            Implementation strategies for TQM
            Conclusion

Chapter 7... **Page 64**
    AVISO: An Innovative Interlibrary Loan Management
    System .... *Dave Binkley*
            Overview
            AVISO: History and Structure
            Interlibrary Loan Process
            AVISO Files
            Verification
            Messaging
            Circulation
            Accounting
            Conclusion

Chapter 8 .... **Page 77**
    Sweeping Sand at the Sea: The Challenge of Staffing a
    Growing Service .... *Kathryn J. Deiss*
        Introduction
        Interlibrary Loan, a Positive Driving Force
        Technological Change
        Changes in Work Patterns and Job Responsibility
        Nontechnological Changes
        Changes in Work Relationships
        Staff Training in a Changing Environment
        Changes in Staffing Levels
        Leadership in Managing Interlibrary Loan
        Conclusion

Chapter 9 .... **Page 86**
    Managing Interlibrary Loan Operations: A Successful Experience
    in an Academic Library .... *Martha Steele and Keiko Horton*
        Introduction
        Subjective Task Analysis
        Total Quality Management
        Value Analysis
        Case Study
        Managing Working Flow
        Interdepartmental Functions
        Physical Arrangement Accommodating the Work Flow
        Impact of Computer Technology
        Conclusion

Chapter 10 .... **Page 97**
    The Leading/Bleeding Edge: The Role/Toll Of Library Staff
    Involved in Electronic Resource Sharing .... *Sheila Walters*
        Introduction
        Impact of Information Technology on Library Staff
        Information Technology
        Challenges in Electronic Database Access
        Electronic Access and Interlibrary Loan
        Reciprocal Agreement Among Libraries
        Commercial Document Services
        New Role in ILL/DDS Staffing
        Resource Sharing and ILL/DDS
        Conclusion

Chapter 11 .... **Page 112**
    A Cost Analysis for Interlibrary Loan : A
    Differentiated Service .... *Amy Chang*
        Introduction
        Cost Studies
        Borrowing Cost vs. Purchasing
        Quality vs. Quantity
        Intangible vs. Tangible
        Conclusion

Chapter 12 .... **Page 116**
    Interlibrary Loan : A Cooperative Effort Among
    OCLC Users .... *Kate Nevins and Darryl Lang*
        Introduction
        Growth in Borrowing and Lending on the OCLC ILL System
        Borrowing and Lending by Type of Library
        Borrowing and Lending by Type of State
        Conclusion

Index .... **Page 123**

Foreword

In today's electronic age, information technologies have revolutionized the traditional way of acquiring research materials and yielded demands for high-speed document delivery. This new information climate creates greater needs for resource sharing among libraries and just-in-time delivery service and shifts interlibrary loan (ILL) to the front line of information delivery. In this ever-changing electronic environment, ILL managers and librarians must not only maximize the access to resource sharing networks locally and nationally, but also utilize numerous electronic document delivery options to satisfy the needs for information on demand. Simultaneously, costs for ILL must be managed and controlled, new technologies must be adapted and implemented, staffing must be trained and re-trained, services must be customized for clienteles, and copyright, policies, and agreements must be complied with. ILL also has entered the era in which ILL competes with commercial document delivery services in the information market. Clearly, coordinating Resource Sharing and managing ILL operations are more challenging than ever before. Having faced this dilemma, some librarians see limitations, while others envision new opportunities to advance resource sharing.

With this awareness, "Managing Resource Sharing in the Electronic Age" focuses on two major issues that have transformed the landscape of ILL in the 1990s: ILL management and electronic/commercial document delivery. Curtis L. Kendrick articulates the core competencies of ILL, while Yem Siu Feng details the evolution of ILL electronic technologies. These two chapters unfold two themes for this volume.

In the section on document delivery, Lee Anne George, Rosann Bazirjian, Pamela W. McLaughlin, and Mary A. Hollerich offer their expertise and knowledge of the utilization electronic/commercial document delivery. Authors also analyze the information market for commercial document delivery. In the management section, Amy Chang focuses on Total Quality Management, Dave Binkley introduces the AVISO system, an innovative database management system for ILL; Kathryn J. Deiss, Martha Steele, Keiko Horton, and Sheila Walters further discuss management challenges in the electronic age. Authors also share ideas and successful experiences in managing the complexity of service activities and stress the impact of new technologies on ILL operations and services. Cost effectiveness is the key factor in managing ILL. In her essay, Amy Chang analyzes cost elements for a differentiated ILL service.

As libraries face substantial increases in ILL, there is no consolidated data to reflect the nationwide ILL activity. However, dual data from ILL OCLC sustains the resource-sharing effort among libraries. Kate Nevins and Darryl Lang provide the rapid growth rate between the fiscal years of 1986 to 1991. The high volume reflects vast demands for global information access. Their studies by type of library and by states indicate the ever-increasing need for resource sharing from coast to coast.

These chapters present how ILL managers and librarians have adapted to economic and technological changes; how reengineering and redesigning have already been undertaken; and how increasing demands were filled with limited resources in the 1990s. ILL managers and librarians' leading efforts provide momentum to today's resource sharing and document delivery. Their vision of information service lays a solid foundation for tomorrow's information delivery.

Amy Chang

THE COMPETITIVE ADVANTAGE OF LIBRARIANS: CORE COMPETENCIES FOR DOCUMENT DELIVERY

Curtis L. Kendrick
Assistant Director in the University
Library for the Depository
Harvard University Library

INTRODUCTION

Technological developments and economic pressures of the recent past have led to the emergence of a new industry, the document delivery industry. What is unique about this industry is the diversity of its firms and institutions, ranging from for-profit enterprises to non-profit organizations, and including a significant number of joint ventures drawing upon both ends of the spectrum.[1] For librarians, the emergence of the document delivery industry has been met with both eager anticipation and trepidation. The opportunity presented by the larger societal focus on how information is created, organized, stored, and disseminated bears the commensurate risk that the significant issues of the day largely will be resolved by others. In the face of this new competition, librarians have certain core competencies that may provide a competitive advantage in the document delivery industry. According to Porter, competitive advantage derives from the value a firm or institution creates for its clients. Competitive advantage "may take the form of prices lower than the competitors' for equivalent benefits or the provision of unique benefits that more than offset a premium price."[2] The extent to which librarians can influence the basis of competition to coincide with our professional capabilities and concerns may largely determine our ability to compete successfully as providers of document delivery services

DOCUMENT DISTRIBUTION CHAIN

The movement of documents from creation to utilization can be viewed as a distribution chain comprising several nodes (Fig. 1.1):

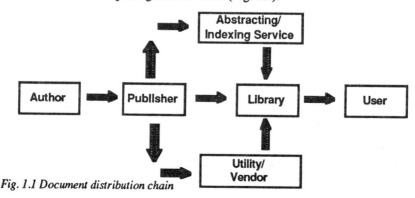

Fig. 1.1 Document distribution chain

1

Driven primarily by technological change, the traditional roles played by each node in the document distribution chain are being challenged. In the future, fewer nodes will be required. For example, direct author-to-user communication is already taking place, most prominently on the Internet, though such direct distribution will not dominate in the near future. What is occurring today is a competitive positioning among the nodes as institutions seek to reengineer the process by which documents are distributed to users. For librarians, what this restructuring means is that for the first time we are witnessing competition in our core business of providing information to end users.

Traditionally, academic libraries have had a monopoly (or at least operated as a cartel) for providing the information services delivered on campus. Competition between institutions has existed, but indirectly and framed by collegiality. The libraries of Brown and Emory universities may compare notes about the size of their collections, but both share similar perspectives about their role within the institution as the main source of information for students, a key source of information for faculty, and a means to develop collections that will support research well into the future. There has been a nonarticulated understanding among institutions that, while competitive, academic libraries have similar values, objectives, and constraints. Document delivery providers from the private or quasi-private sector have a different set of values, where service is subordinate to profit, or at least to revenue. These differences have resulted in an exacerbation of the traditional tensions between libraries and for-profit institutions, and the development of document delivery services to date is reflective of a fundamental dichotomy of purpose.

THREE PERSPECTIVES ON DOCUMENT DELIVERY

For libraries, the main economic impetus for the development of document delivery services has been the obscene escalation of serial prices over the past decade. Librarians have initiated document delivery services in conjunction with serial cancellation projects. In the library view of document delivery, private firms are just one source of material the library provides to its users. Private-sector firms have appeared on the document delivery landscape as a result of technological innovations that enable them to market services directly to users. In the private- sector view of docu-

Fig. 1.2. Library view of document delivery

2

ment delivery, libraries are just one of many clients. Users, at the same time, have become more aggressive in asserting their requirements for information delivery that is fast, convenient, and economical, regardless of its source. In the user view of document delivery, the source of the information is transparent—whoever can get it there the quickest, most conveniently, and cheapest will get the business. These three views of document delivery are depicted in Fig. 1.2-4.

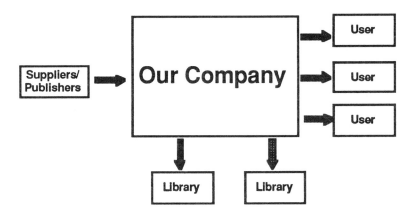

Fig 1.3. Vendor view of document delivery

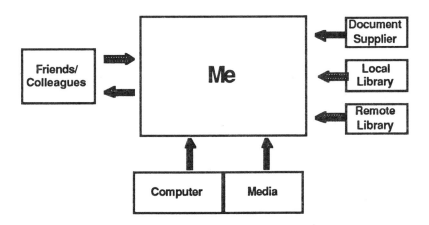

Fig 1.4. User view of document delivery

3

CRITICAL SUCCESS FACTORS FOR DOCUMENT DELIVERY

While these figures represent three different perspectives on document delivery, the perspective of the users is the one that matters. The decisions of end users on how to acquire information will ultimately determine the outcome of the competition between libraries and their for-profit counterparts. From a user perspective, the critical success factors of a document delivery program include availability of material, price, speed, and convenience. A successful document delivery service must provide the material users want in a fashion that is convenient, quick, and reasonably priced. These are the factors by which users currently gauge the utility of document delivery systems. To compete successfully, librarians must meet user performance requirements along these dimensions. This requires reshaping the competitive landscape to align more closely with those areas in which librarians are able to position themselves in a competitive advantage.

On the basis of availability of materials, libraries enjoy a significant advantage compared to commercial firms, but the ability to sustain this advantage is now in question. "There is a very dangerous contradiction here: as information becomes more specialized and more expensive, libraries are less able to develop coherent and comprehensive collections. These same forces cause the consumers of knowledge to choose to pay for private access (e.g., creating private libraries, or using fee for service online information resources), and be less willing to support the library as a "free" information commons." Academic libraries offer a breadth and depth of collections unmatched by commercial firms. Beyond local collections, traditional interlibrary loan has promised users access to an open universe of all publications, and fill rates exceeding 90 percent are not uncommon. Most commercial document delivery services are less ambitious and provide access to a restricted list of titles going back for a limited time. Many of the for-profit document delivery suppliers offer access to 10,000 to 20,000 serial and periodical titles, a small portion of the world's output. For example, the selection criteria for OCLC's ArticleFirst and ContentsFirst databases are "that the titles be primarily in the English language and that they have a publication frequency greater than annual." To limit this universe still further, OCLC only includes titles covered by the major indexing and abstracting services and titles that are held by ninety or more libraries according to the OCLC Holdings file.

That libraries have more extensive holdings does not alone provide a competitive advantage for document delivery. From a user perspective, that the library holds x million volumes may be terrific, but what really matters is the subset of that collection that is of use to the individual. Several document delivery alternatives have taken advantage of this by offering a discipline-based critical mass of publications. The ADONIS system, for example, provides CD-ROM access to about forty leading titles in biomedicine and biotechnology. Along with the annual licensing fee, a charge is incurred each time an article is printed. With limited time, many users will have the inclination to use those sources that promise to "make sense" of the vast universe of information, even, perhaps, if out-of-pocket expenses are incurred.

The determination of what comprises core services (free to users) and what comprises premium services (user fees) varies from institution to institution. One of the

4

traditional roles of the library has been to serve as what Lewis has called the information subsidy of the community. User fees, if any, have served to ration services rather than recover costs. The price charged for a particular service has been set with virtual independence of the cost of providing the service. Compared to commercial firms, libraries tend to be labor intensive and have rigid budget cycles and high overhead. While it may cost libraries more than commercial firms to provide document delivery services, libraries can still compete on the basis of price charged to users by providing a subsidy to the user community. It is critical, however, that librarians know the true cost of the services being provided.

The cost study of interlibrary loan conducted by the Research Libraries Group and the Association of Research Libraries provides information that may be of use to both librarians and users[6]. The cost of an interlibrary loan transaction has led some to consider using commercial sources instead of interlibrary loan. While this may be an appropriate response, such analysis must move beyond simple unit cost comparisons. The entire, fully allocated cost of document delivery alternatives needs to be assessed, which includes start up costs such as hardware, software, subscriptions, and training. For example, the document delivery services supported by RLG and OCLC, as well as UMI's ProQuest Power Pages system, are all excellent services with favorable unit cost structures. However, initial start up costs can easily run into several tens of thousands of dollars.

"Collection-based document suppliers (such as UMI and UnCover) only deal with the well verified materials that they are known to own. If that were the case here in my own lending operation, our costs would be a heck of a lot lower. By collection-based suppliers siphoning off more and more of what I see as the easy ILL requests, that means that ILL offices will be dealing more and more with difficult requests. We may see a decrease in the lending volume but it may well have little impact on staffing because what is coming in is so much more demanding."[7]

A common image of document delivery services is of documents being faxed within hours of a request, or being sped along the Internet direct to a user's workstation. Throughput time—the time from which a user identifies an item of interest until that item (or a representation thereof) is in the user's hands—is certainly critical. Perhaps no less important, however, is the flexibility to customize speed of delivery to correspond with the requirements of the individual user. Ideally, a document delivery system should offer the flexibility of trading off speed for lower price, or trading up for more speed by paying a bit more. Cawkell expresses this concept as follows: "The curious fact is that, to the best of my knowledge, no effort has been made to assess the value of 'speed'. What kind of publication, available from libraries, is wanted by what kind of people, and what would be the added value of receiving it in one hour or overnight?"[8]

A final critical success factor for document delivery is convenience. While libraries may not be easy to use, they are predictable and reliable. Many of the skills developed while learning to use one library can readily be transferred to another. As options for document delivery emerge, users will ask questions about the ease of use of each system and will require options for delivery format—fax, workstation, hard copy. An important criterion will be the ease with which both library staff and users can incorporate a particular service or technology into their daily routines, what Jackson has called work flow integration[9]. Another aspect of convenience is the similarity of user interfaces across systems. As systems support more complex features, the ability of the user interface to be intuitive typically declines. Consequently, additional training and documentation are required.

Competition for document delivery services in the electronic age is currently based upon convenience, speed, price, and availability of material. While librarians certainly need to develop services that can be competitive against all of these factors, the reality is that libraries are saddled with organizational and cost structures that inhibit the ability to provide information inexpensively, conveniently, and quickly. The bureaucratic nature of libraries tends to retard the development of new services and technologies, or, more precisely, new services and technologies must coexist with those they seek to replace. Libraries cannot simply shut down operations that no longer fit within the strategic focus of the organization. For-profit organizations are more flexible in implementing wide- scale changes and are able to capitalize quickly on new opportunities. The following is a list of issues with which UCLA had to contend during the planning process for its document delivery service. UCLA's experience is likely not atypical; however, it exemplifies the difficulties in implementing change within large, complex, and bureaucratic institutions:[10]

1. The campus must determine who falls into the on-campus category of library users and who does not.
2. The campus must register users to assure their eligibility, define user class, and guard the campus against bad debts.
3. Users must be made aware of copyright rules and must indicate that they will obey them by signing a compliance statement.
4. The campus must agree about which materials are to be made available for delivery.
5. The campus must decide on centralized or decentralized service. UCLA has four interlibrary loan centers and nineteen separate libraries.
6. The campus must decide on the fees to be charged.

So much simpler just to dial up a request on the Internet and enter a credit card number.

At present, no single organization—academic or private sector—has been able to develop a sustainable competitive advantage in all of the critical success factors for document delivery. Some institutions or firms have chosen to optimize for speed, others for price, others for availability of material. No one entity has yet been able to put together the entire package. Consequently, there is a common sentiment within the profession that so far, document delivery has been more smoke and mirrors than real documents being delivered to real people. The OCLC Reference Services/Electronic Publishing Interest Group has identified several reasons why the utilization of document delivery services has not yet become widespread:[11]

1. Interlibrary loan is still cheaper.
2. There is growing use of cooperative agreements among libraries.
3. The timeliness of document delivery is not as important as once thought.
4. Campus politics with faculty does not encourage many cancellations of journals.
5. Budget cuts have not reached deep enough.
6. Document suppliers do not carry expensive, hard-to-find items that are being borrowed on ILL now.
7. Libraries are more liberal in interpreting copyright laws.
8. Abstracts are not available on most [online] indexes, so the risk is high in ordering an item that might not really be wanted.
9. The convenience factor for those people who are connected is still relatively unknown.

CORE COMPETENCIES FOR DOCUMENT DELIVERY

While the reality of document delivery has perhaps not yet lived up to the heat generated in the professional literature and at conferences, there is a palpable excitement of potential energy. What is exciting, what has caused librarians to become intoxicated by the allure of the idea of document delivery, is the challenge of competition. More than just competition, here, finally, is a battle that can be won. After years of spiraling serial costs, acute staff cuts, and ever constraining budgetary guidelines,. . . well, damn it, providing information to people — that is our job!

Perhaps. Librarians do have a set of competencies and values through which a competitive advantage in the delivery of documents to users may be developed and sustained. These include user confidence, equity of access, privacy, copyright, and resource sharing. Insofar as these issues are important to users—to the extent that they are "valued" in the marketplace, librarians will be successful in competing to provide document delivery services.

A key advantage enjoyed by libraries in the competition to serve as document delivery suppliers is the generally high degree of confidence users have in the library as an institution. As noted earlier, this confidence is fundamentally based upon elements of predictability and reliability. With much accuracy, a user can predict the type of services he or she is likely to receive within a library. Similarly, users have certain expectations for the quality of services received — they may not like that it might take two weeks to receive an item on interlibrary loan, but this does not generally come as a surprise. The challenge is to expand users' view of what constitutes basic library service and to align service capabilities more closely with users' needs.

As a group, libraries have an advantage over any single commercial firm in that we have a huge installed user base. The decision by an individual user to procure documents from a source external to the library bears some degree of risk. Users have little knowledge of the credibility of the firm or in the viability of the technology a particular company may use to supply documents. Absent a strong motivation (price, speed, convenience) to obtain documents from an external source, users will be inclined to continue to use and regard the library as their main source of documents.

While professionally and personally we may value the idea of equal access for all to information, this ideal is unlikely ever to be a reality in our market-driven society. As with health care and legal services, the ability to obtain the highest caliber of information services will likely continue to depend largely on one's financial resources. Ensuring that people with limited economic and technical resources still have access to critical information, however, should be a fundamental value shared by all within our profession. "Librarians stand at the focal point for support of the free flow of information; access is a fundamental value for the profession."[12] Traditionally, librarians' roles in the process of promoting access have been on the back end—making people aware that information exists and developing systems by which the information is conveyed to users. Increasingly, librarians will also have a vital role to play by assessing user needs for information and conveying these needs to information creators.

Confidentiality has long been a trademark of librarianship. "At least 38 states have enacted legislation to protect the confidentiality of data included in patron records, legally vesting library staff with the responsibility for securing from unauthorized access information about individual library users."[13] Librarians can help to ensure that the information-using behavior of users is not bartered, broadcast, or sold. "The lack of strong legislative guarantees, combined with the difficulty of enforcement has created an information policy environment where privacy is far from guaranteed."[14] It is worth noting that even aggregated data about usage have commercial value. Currently, librarians are giving this information away as part of licensing agreements that require article-level detail of usage patterns. As articles have replaced journal issues as the information currency of exchange, commercial firms and publishers have much greater detail about what sells. Insofar as economic concerns dictate what gets published, the world of information may become more narrow, as only articles on marketable topics get published.

Libraries have an advantage over commercial document providers under copyright law. This advantage results from the fact that, typically, libraries do not make a profit from their document delivery activities. In addition, copyright law specifically allows resource sharing by libraries through interlibrary loan.[15] Since the 1976 Copyright Act, the law has lagged behind technological developments. The law continues to evolve through legislation and litigation, and it is critical that librarians work to ensure that the primary purpose of copyright remains to promote the progress of science and the useful arts, not to make sure that the right people get paid. The (TRLN) Copyright Policy Task Force has proposed a model whereby ownership of intellectual property would remain with individuals and institutions.[16] Such initiatives are worth pursuing, if only for the leverage that might accrue to institutions. "Time is short for universities to reestablish themselves as controllers of the information stock they themselves create. Once commercial publishers recognize that universities might attempt to reestablish their rightful role in scholarly communication, they will undoubtedly try to subvert the effort. They currently have significant economic leverage over librarians and our faculty, and they have the momentum of the status quo behind them."[17]

More than just the status quo, publishers have the law behind them, and they have launched an offensive through litigation. The body of case law that is emerging pertaining to fair use is based mostly upon private sector examples, thus allowing publishers to "define narrowly the boundaries of fair use especially when university legal counsels tend to urge cautious responses to the threat of litigation."[18] Perhaps it would be useful if a group of institutions were to step forward with an aggressive interpretation of users' rights under copyright and a willingness to pursue matters through the process of litigation.

A final area in which libraries enjoy a significant competitive advantage over commercial firms is in resource sharing. We have a professional predisposition to share with one another—information, collections, services and people—that is unique. A relatively recent trend within the private sector has been the development of the network organizational model within industries. For example, the interrelationships that developed among firms in Silicon Valley during the 1980s have been characterized as epitomizing a network organization.[19] Libraries have been building networks for decades to enable and support the sharing of resources. "Approximately two-thirds of a century ago, during the depths of the Depression, administrators, faculty, and librarians at Duke and UNC-CH [University of North Carolina-Chapel Hill] realized that they would never have enough money to build two separate comprehensive collections. By working together, however, TRLN librarians have built coordinated, interdependent, and interlocked collections of far greater breadth and depth than they could have achieved alone."[20]

The defining characteristics of an industry or a subset of an industry that is arranged as a network are that the locus of control is external to any institution, an institution is able only to influence outcomes rather than to determine them, and the institution is shaped by its people, rather than its corporate requirements. A network organization requires resource sharing because no single firm is adequately able to function independently. Virtually all institutions would prefer to be self-sufficient; institutions turn to a network when it becomes clear that self-sufficiency is not an option. The advantage of a network organizational model is that it allows for a specialization of roles around common goals. Scale economies can be achieved through shared activities. The keys to success include cooperation, shared risk, and shared benefit, not greed.

The sharing of resources required for document delivery services suggests that libraries need to build and expand upon existing local, national, and international networks. The range of issues with which we must contend is too broad, the substance too complex, and the resources too scarce for any single institution to be self-sufficient. While collections are an important resource to be shared within the network, "networking places a new emphasis on personnel. Power, expertise, perceived trustworthiness and social bonds are often person-specific rather than firm-specific."[21] Every institution has unique characteristics that enable it to do certain things well, other things less well. These characteristics are most directly the function of the individuals who comprise the organization. Under a network organization for document delivery, the diversity of skills required to meet current and future challenges will be emphasized within the network at large. Local institutions will rely on a skill set that is external to the organization, but which allows each participant to contribute what they can and to draw from it what they need. Under this model, resource sharing will move beyond collection development: some libraries will function as central repositories; others will develop technologies for storing, accessing, and disseminating information; others still will develop expertise at communicating with users, negotiating contracts, and managing services. As Wessling has noted, "[i]f libraries act cooperatively and aggressively to expand document delivery options, they will prove that they can plan a leadership role in meeting the information needs of users in the 1990s."[22]

FROM MASS MARKETING TO RELATIONSHIP MARKETING

The continued evolution of the network organizational model for academic libraries is consistent with how research practitioners have organized themselves. Due primarily to continued specialization, researchers typically employ a network of colleagues both internal and external to their local institutions. In the highly competitive domain of academia, researchers take care to nurture relationships with those they trust to expand their personal and professional networks. While institutional loyalty is still important, it is subordinate to the personal networks that individual researchers have established. The primacy of the individual over the institution has ramifications for libraries. The key challenge will be for academic libraries to become part of a researcher's network. This cannot be done by the mass marketing of services; rather, it requires a more personalized approach, what has been called relationship marketing.

With relationship marketing, the process by which transactions occur is elevated to equal status with the commodity being exchanged. This approach is increasingly being taken in the professional-services sector where the detailed knowledge required of the specialist far exceeds the interest and ability of most lay persons to comprehend. Specialists are finding that spending time fostering a personal and individualized relationship with clients helps to establish trust and confidence. As patients share confidential medical histories with doctors, or as clients share details of their legal situation with attorneys, so too may researchers come to entrust their information needs with librarians. Building upon the elements of user confidence and our reputation for confidentiality, librarians may come to play a central role within an individual researcher's network. By developing one-on-one relationships with scholars, librarians will be able to tailor services to meet individual needs. Moreover, librarians will be better positioned to shape user expectations for what libraries can provide and to help users understand the potential tradeoffs among their options for document delivery.

CONCLUSION

The flow of information from creation to utilization can be viewed as a distribution chain comprising several interacting nodes, with each node fulfilling a mix of specialized or general roles. What we are witnessing now can be called role re-specification in the document distribution chain, as new relationships, technologies, and economies are challenging the old. There is much fluidity and ambiguity at the present time, and much overlap is occurring among the various entities competing to serve as document providers. Currently, competition is on the basis of price, speed of delivery, convenience, and availability of materials. While libraries need to maintain a competitive position with respect to these factors. They may lose their advantage along some of these dimensions to competitors from the for-profit sector. Libraries have a unique advantage over for-profit firms in the areas of user confidence, ensuring access, privacy, confidentiality, copyright, and resource sharing. To the extent that these areas become key factors in user decisions about how to acquire documents, they will provide a sustainable competitive advantage for librarians within the document delivery industry.

References

1. There is a dizzying array of document delivery providers ranging from campus sneaker-net services to digital imaging projects. Some of the vendors include the Research Libraries Group, Online Computer Library Center, British Library Document Supply Center, University Microfilms, Inc., Article Express, Genuine Article, UnCover, Faxon, TULIP Project, and ADONIS. The typology is clouded by the fact that many of the document delivery services offered by non-profit agencies share characteristics with those offered by commercial firms, and some of the products vended by the for-profits are distributed through libraries. For the purposes of this essay, the distinction is made between library based services drawing upon local collections or resource sharing agreements (ILL) and the group of newer entrants to the document delivery industry.

2. Michael E. Porter, *Competitive Advantage: Creating and Sustaining Superior Performance*, New York: Free Press 1985, xvi.

3. Peter Lyman, "Can Higher Education Afford Research Libraries?" Library Hi Tech 10, no.3 (1992). p. 76.

4. Nancy Campbell, "OCLC's New Serials Databases, ArticleFirst and ContentsFirst," OCLC Newsletter (Mar./Apr., 1993): 22.

5. David W. Lewis, "New Role for Reference Librarians," paper presented the NELINET Reference Technology Advisory Committee Conference, Worcester, MA, April 1993.

6. Marilyn M. Roche. ARL/RLG Interlibrary Loan Cost Study: An Effort by the Association of Research Libraries and the Research Libraries Group. Association of Research Libraries, June 1993. The study found that the average cost to loan an item is $11, to borrow $19.

7. Wayne A. Pedersen, Posting to ILL-L Interlibrary Loan Discussion Group, 27 May, 1993.

8. Cawkell, "Progress in Documentation: Electronic Document Delivery Systems," Journal of Documentation, 47, no. 1 (1991): 42.

9. Mary E. Jackson, "Resource Sharing and Document Delivery in the 1990s," Wilson Library Bulletin (Feb. 1993): 36.

10. Dennis E. Smith and Clifford A. Lynch, "An Overview of Document Delivery Systems at the University of California," Journal of Interlibrary Loan & Information Supply 2, no 2 (1991): 25.

11. *OCLC Users Council Meeting Minutes, February 7-9, 1993.*

12. Mary Lou Goodyear, "Information Policy for Electronic Information Resources," The Public Access Computer Systems Review 4, no.6 (1993): 26.

13. Kathleen G. Fouty, "Online Patron Records and Privacy: Service vs. Security," The Journal of Academic Librarianship, 19, no.5 (1993): 289, citing "Confidentiality of Library Records," Newsletter on Intellectual Freedom 37 (Jan. 1988).

14. Goodyear, 27.

15. *U.S. Code Title 17 Sections 108(a) and 108(g).*

16. The Copyright Policy Task Force of the   , *Model University Policy Regarding Faculty Publication in Scientific and Technical Scholarly Journals: A Background Paper and Review of the Issues.* July 1993.

17. Paul Metz and Paul M. Gherman, "Serials Pricing and the Role of the Electronic Journal," College & Research Libraries (July 1991): 326.

18. Duane E. Webster, "Promoting the Principles of Copyright," ARL Newsletter (July 1993): 1.

19. AnnaLee Saxenian, "Regional Networks and the Resurgence of Silicon Valley," California Management Review (Fall 1990): 89 - 112.

20. Patricia Buck Dominguez and Luke Swindler, "Cooperative Collection Development at the   : A Model for the Nation," College & Research Libraries (Nov. 1993): 489.

21. Hans B. Thorelli, "Networks: Between Markets and Hierarchies," Strategic Management Journal 7 (1986)

22. Julie Wessling, "Document Delivery: A Primary Service for the Nineties," in *Advances in Librarianship Volume 16.* Edited by M. J. Voigt (New York, Academic Press, 1991): 1.

FROM PAPER FORMS TO ELECTRONIC TRANSMISSION: THE EVOLUTION OF INTERLIBRARY LOAN ELECTRONIC TECHNOLOGIES

Yem Siu Fong
Head of Information Delivery Services
University of Colorado

INTRODUCTION

It is an undeniable fact that the world we live in has become increasingly focused on electronic technologies. As library professionals we are bombarded daily by prognostications about the "electronic village," the "information super highway," "virtual collections," and the "digital library." It is the topic of choice in our journals, our e-mail, and our listservs. The most consistent vision of information delivery is one that describes the delivery of digital files of all kinds, including text, graphics, still images, moving images, and audio to the user's desktop. The interfaces are seamless to the user as digitized, compressed bits are transmitted across high-speed fiber optic cables, and documents are ultimately delivered through various output options. Given a scenario that promises immediate access to globally connected information resources with the corresponding speedy delivery of the requested item, the question is no longer how new technology will effect document delivery, but how new technology will be used to transform traditional interlibrary loan (ILL) into an enhanced, responsive, and comprehensive library document delivery service.

According to statistics gathered by the Association of Research Libraries (ARL) for the years 1985-/-1986 and 1990-/-1991, ILL lending activity increased by 45 percent and borrowing activity by 47 percent[1]. Enhanced availability of bibliographic information via electronic media, such as CD-ROMs, table of contents indexes on OPAC's, and dial-up or Internet connections to library catalogs, have driven the demand for documents upward. At the same time, electronic publishing and the expansion of telecommunication networks are creating rising expectations from information users. Information demand has driven access by electronic advancements, which places ILL and document delivery in the forefront of the new "infostructure" occurring in libraries. We are seeing a definite change in ILL as it moves from a library-to-library process to a patron-initiated one, "with comprehensive access to documents from a variety of sources."[2] Interlibrary loan has historically relied on a wide array of communication and delivery mechanisms to support the borrowing and lending of materials. Today, the convergence of information technologies that allow various systems and networks to communicate is moving ILL into a changed information world. Library professionals are re-thinking and re-evaluating traditional ILL and asking: What are these technological advances? How can links be created between users and document suppliers? How are these changing ILL services in an access-oriented environment? How do we manage technological change advantageously

13

within the context of reduced library budgets and limited resources?

With these questions in mind, this essay focuses on the evolution of information technology applications for enhanced interlibrary loan and will offer suggested models as possible answers to some of these questions. However, to be definitive when describing technological advancements is nearly impossible, as product life cycles shorten and new possibilities constantly appear on the horizon. It is safe to say that we are in an era of unpredictable change with an ever-expanding number of choices. What is true today may easily be reconfigured tomorrow.

HISTORICAL OVERVIEW

Technology has been a growing component of libraries for the past thirty years. Unquestionably, automation of the card catalog revolutionized library operations. For ILL, applications of technology developed piecemeal with very little integration of systems between large bibliographic utilities and local operations.

Traditionally ILL has been a library-to-library service. Local ILL departments assume the responsibility of determining that a document exists and identifying libraries that own the requested item. Both borrowing and lending departments typically use a combination of manual, facsimile, and online ILL messaging systems to process ILL requests. Tasks include: verify citations; locate lenders by searching print and online local, regional, and national catalogs; submit the request to a holding library—sending article specific and requesting library information, and transmitting responses, renewals, and other messages; receive delivery material accompanied by lending messages (i.e., date shipped, due date, etc.); manage the process including tracking status of requests, mailing, billing, and gathering statistics. ILL librarians have long sought computer-based solutions for managing these activities that require following numerous paper trails.

As automation evolved, ILL managers experimented with early messaging systems—sending requests over telephone lines using teletype machines in the mid-1960s and using library-to-library terminal connections in the 1970s. In the 1980s, many libraries cooperated in developing local and regional messaging software, often e-mail based, and utilizing a variety of telecommunication channels. As a result, in the 1990s message formats vary among library networks and utilities.

During the 1980s, this proliferation of computer applications prompted ILL managers to establish national and international ILL standards and to address the issue of multiple formats. There are national standards for ILL data elements and ILL protocols approved by the International Standardization Organization (ISO). The ILL protocol for exchanging ILL messages such as requests, renewals, and cancellations was approved in 1991 as an international standard by the ISO.[3] As technological changes occur in an open, distributive setting, defining standards will continue to be important. Historically, utilities like OCLC and RLIN have often set de facto standards as they developed ILL systems.

14

OCLC

The promise of a national online system that would automate many ILL functions became reality when OCLC, the Online Computer Library Center, activated its first ILL system in 1979. Most significantly, OCLC paved the way for electronic messaging systems in other major utilities and engineered links between bibliographic information in its online union catalog with the online requesting and messaging component. The ILL system transfers bibliographic data into an online ILL template and inserts standard borrower information. A borrower-generated string of five institutions allows requests to be transmitted sequentially to each lender if the one before cannot fill the request. The first OCLC ILL system was an early step toward one-stop verification and location of an item, replacing hours of searching printed indexes, union lists, and library catalogs.

As OCLC developed into the largest bibliographic utility in the U.S., adding Library of Congress MARC tapes, member records, British Library titles, and international libraries' holdings, it became a powerful source for verifying titles and locating owners of material.

In 1994 OCLC contained over 27 million bibliographic records and had more than 5,500 libraries participating in the ILL system. Over 7 million loan transactions had been filled by its 5,500 members, with 55 million requests logged by the end of 1993. By the end of 1994[4] The ILL Micro Enhancer software made it possible to process routine tasks, such as the updating of ILL records, in batch mode. The program supports the printing of barcoded numbers that can be scanned for faster entry of ILL record numbers. Increased efficiencies such as the Micro Enhancer are reasons many libraries continue to rely on OCLC to support the majority of ILL operations. Other advantages of OCLC include access to online ILL policy information and serials union list holdings and production of statistical reports. According to OCLC PRISM ILL Report of 1994, ninety percent of the requests made via the OCLC ILL system are filled, 86% by the first or second lender.

In December 1992, OCLC introduced the PRISM ILL system, which offers numerous enhancements, including a greater degree of flexibility in editing features of the ILL and workform, new borrowing fields and field lengths, etc. PRISM ILL provides the advantage of searching by keywords and boolean operators. It also links FirstSearch databases with the end-user, offers full-text articles, and provides an option to request items through the local ILL service.

Other library utilities have also developed ILL subsystems, including the Research Libraries Information Network (RLIN), Washington Library Network (WLN), and the National Library of Medicine's (NLM) Docline network.

ILL MANAGEMENT

While utilities have contributed to automating ILL functions, there are still missing links between these ILL systems and local ILL management. In setting the stage for a new information future, Shirley Baker and Mary Jackson, in an ARL white paper on interlibrary loan, address the need for locally managed ILL systems able to import and export data from a variety of sources, such as online catalogs, OCLC, gateways to document suppliers.[5] Their white paper has resulted in an initiative of the Association of Research Libraries, known as the North American Interlibrary Loan/ Document Delivery (NAILDD) Project. "The mission of this Project is to streamline and redesign traditional ILL systems while moving toward a user-initiated requesting environment."[6]

While the need for electronic document delivery for the future is emphasized, it is also true that many ILL requests can only be filled by other libraries. A large portion of scholarly information, particularly in the humanities and social sciences, will not be available in electronic formats. Advocates of the new vision for ILL propose an enhanced service that incorporates traditional ILL while offering a variety of other document delivery alternatives for the end user[7]. These alternatives include traditional resource sharing models, reliance on ILL systems, patron-initiated ordering, and commercial document delivery.

In the current state of flux, libraries must deal with the impact of technological change as it affects the allocation of resources and the development and setting of new information access policies. Who will manage these technologically driven developments? How will libraries shift personnel and train staff as well as users? Many libraries are seeking answers by implementing pilot projects. An increasingly popular application is to provide avenues for patrons to initiate requests and to receive documents electronically.

MODEL PROJECTS

Electronic Requests

Libraries over the past twenty years have created local or regional electronic ILL request systems, often using e-mail, that allow ILL staff to transmit electronically ILL requests to either their host institution or to other participating lenders through a dedicated terminal or dial-up connection. Replacing paper ILL request forms, a local or cooperative electronic ILL module has the potential for forming the basis of an ILL management system that ideally interfaces with a variety of resources and utilities. These systems can be mounted on local area networks (LAN) and have been proven to improve workflow by providing legible, complete requests. Moreover, the electronic ILL request mechanism becomes increasingly valuable as it is linked to the online bibliographic record, the institution's patron files, and gateways to commercial and outside suppliers.

In the university setting, electronic requesting has often evolved in conjunction with multi-campus or campus-wide document delivery services. The University of California's (CLC) MELVYL system added a REQUEST function in 1992 offering faculty, students, and staff the ability to request articles directly from a search in MELVYL, thus eliminating the need to hard-copy or print citations. Requests are automatically linked to MELVYL call numbers. A user in the multi-campus system designates the campus document requesting service, and the system verifies the eligibility of the user and the account number. Requests are sent to the appropriate service via electronic mail and assigned a mail ID that permits users to check the status of their requests. The UC libraries are considering modifying the request system to support interlibrary loan among the UC campuses. [8]

Several libraries have developed electronic ILL request functions using e-mail applications.[9] Colorado State University (CSU) offers an electronic request system that can be used in three different ways.

1. The basic request program provides a blank template that is menu driven and prompts the user to fill in patron information, including identification number and book or article citation information.
2. An ILL link to CD-ROM databases on the library's LAN is the second component of CSU's electronic ILL. After a user completes a CD-ROM search and decides on needed citations, the user is taken directly into the ILL program, which prompts users to complete brief personal information. The program uploads pertinent bibliographic information, automatically formats it similar to the basic ILL template, and mails the request over the LAN to the ILL office. Known as the "Uplink" program, this software automatically checks the library's holdings and reprints the citation with the library's call number, saving the user and ILL staff time and effort.
3. The "Grab-It" program allows users to access any electronic database via modem or telnet. The needed items can be saved through a screen capture. The patron's information is automatically attached along with the copyright statement, then transmitted via the LAN to the ILL office. Users must request a floppy disk of the program, which limits users to fifteen screens or items per search session.

CSU has tested an e-mail link to OCLC that will automatically load their patron requests into the OCLC ILL system. The requests would reside in a review file and would be processed without re-keying information.

Electronic Delivery

Article citation databases that offer a document delivery component are being marketed directly to end users. Accessible via CD-ROM indexes, OPACS, online services, and Internet gateways, these products allow users to identify needed citations and transmit requests at the point useful references are discovered. The UnCover database offers over 16,000 journals held by contributing libraries and allows users to locate articles by a keyword search of the table of contents. UnCover displays library holdings and issue-specific articles. Users can then purchase a copy of the item, with fax delivery promised within forty-eight hours. Average fees for UnCover are about $11 per document including copyright payment. UnCover is also developing ways to block patrons from ordering articles from locally held journals, paving the way for libraries to consider funding unmediated document delivery.

If libraries are unable to subsidize this service, the ideal electronic ILL system would allow several levels of options for the user. One level would permit users to request electronically to the ILL office or networked lending library. With limited acquisition dollars, many libraries are pursuing resource-sharing arrangements to purchase tapeloads of article citation databases, such as those produced by the Institute for Scientific Information (ISI), or are loading full-text article indexes and databases, such as those offered by Information Access Corporation (IAC). An electronic ILL request function linked to these citation databases would facilitate the ILL process.

With these options on the market, the library no longer serves as the sole intermediary or document delivery option. Article citation databases, such as OCLC's FirstSearch, offer two choices at the point of discovery: the library can receive the request and fill as an ILL, or the user can authorize payment using a credit card and have the request filled by a commercial document supplier, such as UMI or ISI. Libraries that offer FirstSearch have the option of turning on an ILL link. This service permits an end-user to send requests to the ILL office; via a Review file in the PRISM ILL SYSTEM for action by ILL staff.

Recent studies on fee-based document delivery cite average costs to be between $10 and $20 per item, which includes copyright fees. In Colorado, libraries including the University of Colorado at Denver and Colorado State University are subsidizing unmediated document delivery to campus clientele using services such as UnCover and FirstSearch.

Arizona State University (ASU), Rice University, and the University of Colorado library system are among the libraries that have conducted pilot projects to evaluate the use of commercial document delivery vendors. These tests commonly compare cost, turnaround time, quality, and service among vendors by contrasting them with traditional ILL service. Vendors such as UnCover, University Microfilms Inc. (UMI), ISI, and British Library Document Supply Centre (BLDSC) have been evaluated among the suppliers. While libraries find quality and cost acceptable, there are generally limitations in service from commercial vendors as well as gaps in retrospective holdings by organizations whose document delivery holdings only began since the late 1980s. ASU's unpublished study shows that 32 percent of the photocopy requests processed were supplied by commercial vendors, while the remaining were filled by other libraries.

Suppliers such as UMI and ISI will continue to compete in this arena. Their prompt delivery services certainly offer an alternative to users and ILL. In addition to these sources, full-text articles will be another avenue for expedited document delivery to the end-user. The current disadvantage of full-text retrieval is the lack of graphs, charts, and formulae. Full-image document delivery will eliminate this disadvantage.

More and more end-user services produced by library utilities are appearing. RLG's (Research Library Group) CitaDel files include the British Library Document Supply Centre's (BLDSC) Inside Information database, which provides journal citation information for 10,000 of the most often requested titles in BLDSC's collection. EBSCO is developing a new product known as CASIAS (Current Awareness Service, Individual Article Service), which will offer the ability to order articles electronically from suppliers such as BLDSC or from the ADONIS database of over 500 biomedical titles.

These services are continuing to expand, increasing the number of journal titles, and some are adding links to libraries' holdings. Products such as these, which offer "one- stop shopping," also raise policy issues for determining how to subsidize these services and how to shift resources. These issues include re-training staff and offering continuing education in order to stay informed of technological advances. Libraries, especially public institutions, must also confront the "free versus fee" debate when evaluating these products. ILL has traditionally been offered as a free service to provide additional materials outside of a library's collection. If document delivery in an electronic environment is subsidized, libraries will need to decide how to ensure equitable access and whether or not to limit patrons, either by dollar amounts or volume of requests.

CONVERGENT TECHNOLOGIES

Electronic document delivery has evolved in parallel with convergent technologies. These convergent technologies are aptly described by Gary Cleveland and summarized below. A brief summary of points 1, 2, and 4 are included with a discussion on communication technologies presented in the sections that follow.

1. Electronic document conversion, such as scanning or digitizing and electronic generation (i.e., computer-generated text files)
2. Storage technologies
3. Communication technologies
4. Workstation technologies
5. Hardcopy production.[9]

Document imaging technology allows print and microform materials to be transformed into an electronic representation of the physical document. Images are represented by binary codes and may take a variety of formats, differing in complexity, compression, degree of shading, color, and resolution. Various imaging technologies exist, such as fax machines, optical character recognition, and image coding formats, referred to as Group 3 and Group 4 formats.

Magnetic storage technologies including tape, floppy disks, and hard disks are quickly being supplanted by technologies that allow higher density and longer preservation of data without the danger of physical damage or data loss. These technologies include optical storage, CD-ROM, jukebox technology, and magneto-optical disk drives.

Workstations are being developed in what is described as an open architecture, allowing for the interconnectivity of hardware, software, and telecommunications in a distributed, flexible, and changing environment.

Pilot Projects

The Internet has opened up a realm of possibilities for exchanging data and may

19

be used to replace or supplement some existing ILL functions. Electronic mail ILL requests initiated by patrons is one example of an electronic function capable of replacing paper forms. The scanning, digitizing, and compressing of data transmitted over the Internet may replace the photocopying and mailing of articles and offers an alternative to fax transmission. The ability to capture data and images from electronic journals and to use file transfer protocols (FTP) to send articles is an avenue that publishers are exploring, particularly if copyright protection is maintained.

At North Carolina State University (NCSU) a pilot project was conducted from 1991-1992 that integrated electronic requesting, electronic document ordering, and electronic document delivery using the document scanners, the campus file server, the campus network, and the Internet. Users were able not only to conduct searches and identify citations, but also to enter citations into request templates and send them via e-mail to the NCSU libraries where the request was filled either in-house or through ILL. Articles were scanned and transmitted via FTP to the campus file server. The file server used a document server application programmed to place the file in an individual user's account and subsequently sent an e-mail notice to the user. After retrieving the file via FTP and decompressing it, the requester has the option to view the article on screen, print it, create an ASCII file, or pick up a print copy from the library.

A two-year project was conducted by the Ohio State University. The system linked fax machines to microcomputers utilizing Internet transmission. Fax machines acted as scanners with articles being sent over the Internet where they were received by the requesting library's PC, then transmitted to a nearby fax machine for printing hard copies of articles.

These two projects point the way to creating multiple avenues for transmission of data over the Internet. Although there are some perceived disadvantages to the PC fax to fax linkages, the Ohio State project does show how existing technology can be integrated, while the NCSU project provides a model for campus-wide electronic document requesting and delivery. The Colorado Alliance of Research Libraries (CARL) is developing mechanisms for patron-placed holds among participating libraries. This may form the basis for a multi-phase ILL module that will integrate document requesting with interfaces to UnCover, IAC products, ADONIS, UMI's ProQuest, and scanned images coming directly from publishers.[10] The proposed software will support patron-initiated requests electronically and perform routing of these requests, will operate in a workstation environment with connections to utilities such as OCLC, will interface with patron files, will keep management statistics, and will allow local customization and flexibility by participating libraries based on resource-sharing agreements. Conceivably, this module could be used statewide if adapted by the state-supported Access Colorado Library Information Network (ACLIN), which allows users to search remote library catalogs on the Internet.

Electronic Transmission

Sending documents via the Internet is quickly becoming the transmission mode of choice. Whether this is a library-to-library configuration, library-to-patron, or vendor/publisher-to-requester, the flexibility, speed, and quality of digital transmission via fiber optics is providing an innovative method of delivering documents. The Research Libraries Group has developed ARIEL software to support document transmission among libraries.

ARIEL is a product that exemplifies converging technologies, utilizing imaging technology, software to compress text, PC's to store data, and the Internet to transmit the data. Articles are scanned from the original journal page by page. ARIEL software compresses the images to 1/15th of the document's normal size and stores this in the PC. Bit-mapped images are transmitted over the Internet, stored in the receiving library's PC, then printed on a laser printer.

ARIEL is an intermediate step toward document delivery direct to the user's desktop. As with any new technology, the promise of faster delivery of high quality documents must be balanced against the added costs required to implement this technology fully. ARIEL has been shown to provide improved document quality over facsimile. However, libraries have experienced problems such as slow scanning, document loss, and different staffing configurations.

Enhancements of ARIEL allows the software to be used in a more flexible manner with a wider variety of equipment. It operates in a Windows environment, will support a variety of printers, supports all scanners with TWAIN drivers as well as Fujitsu scanners, offers the ability to import foreign Tagged Image File Format (TIFF) files, or files containing images that have not been created directly by ARIEL, provides the ability to view scanned files on screen, and offers increased flexibility in managing ARIEL files, log files, addresses, etc.

MIME

New information technology developments are pointing toward facilitating document delivery in an open systems environment capable of utilizing public domain software and supporting several different brands of hardware. The Multipurpose Internet Mail Extension (MIME) technology allows a variety of document types to be attached to an e-mail message and transmitted between different types of computers and then to be viewed and/or printed. It has been extensively used as a method of delivering graphics files from gophers and World Wide Web servers on the Internet. The system does not rely on file transfer protocols, but could be utilized with a product like ARIEL if the new ARIEL document type is registered as a MIME type.

A proposal authored by Tony Barry of the Australian National University Library outlines the use of standard Internet e-mail technology for interlibrary image transfer and document delivery over the Internet. He categorizes the process into four phases: request, recording, transmission, and receipt:

1. Request enables the user to initiate a request via e-mail to an institution that could fill the request.
2. Recording entails the actual process of scanning a document that results in an image file stored on a hard disk.

21

3. Transmission uses Standard MIME compliant e-mail software to transmit the scanned file back to the requester. Transmission may also include charges or other information. By using Internet remote printing software, tcp.int, a document may be transmitted to a fax machine via the Internet and phone lines.
4. Receipt decodes the image file automatically and saves it to disk. A document could be viewed, printed, saved, or forwarded to an individual with MIME compliant mailer or sent to a fax number for printing.

The advantage of e-mail compliant technology is that it is hardware independent, while ARIEL "relies on both machines at either end, and every part of the link in between, being up and running as it uses a file transfer mechanism."[11] Current examples of MIME compliant software include pine, Eudora, elm, MailManager XLView, Zmail, xmail, mailtool, and Quickmail.

IMPLICATIONS OF TECHNOLOGY

Advancements in e-mail technologies have profoundly changed the way that users can initiate requests and obtain documents using computers. E-mail technologies have also altered how ILL/document delivery departments receive and send requests. However, much remains to be accomplished in applying existing ILL standards and communication protocols to the Internet e-mail environment. As the momentum for a national information infrastructure builds, efforts to regulate these technologies may also develop. A corresponding serious concern is copyright protection in an electronic publishing environment. Publishers, researchers, and scholars are anxious about issues of privacy, authenticity, and proprietary rights issues. As facilitators to information access, libraries need to monitor developments and, at the same time, review current library policies and practices.

Today, administrators face decisions on using limited financial resources to support access. ILL librarians and staff are reevaluating their roles as new technologies change library operations. Users will require assistance and education to understand the significance of new information-access options available to them.

In reality, there will be a population of users who will not have the time or desire to do their own information retrieval, as is already evidenced by the growth of fee-based information services. In addition, there will also be technologically illiterate users, as well as users in geographic locations in which information technology may be unavailable. Information technology is often synonymously associated with economic competitiveness and, as such, leaves economically disadvantaged users or libraries with limited funds out of the picture. Libraries, long champions of serving diverse populations, will be increasingly challenged to provide access and delivery in ways that will be inclusive and fair, and, at the same time, cost effective.

CONCLUSION

Nationally, there have been a number of efforts to develop a national information infrastructure, the goal of which is to transmit massive amounts of information over fiber optic communication lines at high speeds. In this context, information access must be combined with information delivery options. It is no longer realistic to isolate access issues from delivery issues. Due to this change, the new role for ILL/document delivery librarians in the electronic age will be as facilitators to connect users to the information resources using computer technologies.

What we see emerging are models that connect access to distributed online catalogs and citation databases, and local OPACS to multiple document delivery suppliers and other libraries. Local area networks and wide area networks utilizing the Internet will be the communications media of choice. While not discussed in this essay, intelligent agents (i.e., artificial intelligence) may soon become the front-end to our information access as multimedia, video, and audio arrives on users' doorsteps via home cable and satellite. These advancements suggest that there will be a single point of entry by end-users with delivery of information to their desktop.

Patron-initiated electronic document delivery and the integration of traditional ILL with commercial document delivery appear as new service trends. Certainly, libraries are not to the point of fully funding commercial document delivery for their users. However, for those libraries willing to provide financial support, the option of end-user ordering will result in higher fill rates and may moderate increases in ILL volume.

Meeting the new demands of the information age will require planned strategies coordinated among ILL offices, collection management, systems, reference, and other library departments. Providing an expanding range of document delivery services with limited resources will continue to be a major challenge for libraries. Most important electronic access and delivery models cannot be implemented in a vacuum; while maximizing resource sharing opportunities, these new models require policy and operational decisions that will balance library resources.

REFERENCES

1. Tammie N. Dearie and Virginia Steel, *Interlibrary Loan Trends: Staffing and Organization* SPEC Kit #187 (Washington, D.C.: Association of Research Libraries, Office of Management Services, 1992).

2. Julie Wessling, "Document Delivery: A Primary Service for the Nineties," *Advances in Librarianship* 16(1993):1-31.

3. Gary Cleveland, *Electronic Document Delivery: Converging Standards and Technologies*, UDT Series on Data Communication Technologies and Standards for Libraries, Report #2 (Ottawa: IFLA International Office for Universal Dataflow and Telecommunications, 1991).

4. OCLC, "University of Illinois at urbana-Champaign logs 55 millionth OCLC Interlibrary Loan in Record Time," OCLC Press Release, January, 1995.

5. Shirley K. Baker and Mary E. Jackson, Maximizing Access, *Minimizing Cost: A First Step Toward the Information Access Future* (Washington D.C. : Association of Research Libraries, 1992).

6. Association of Research Libraries, *North American Interlibrary Loan/Document Delivery Project*, (Washington, D.C.: Association of Research Libraries, 1993).

7. Wessling, 1-31

8. Gail Ford, *When What You See Is What You Want! UC Berkeley's Experience with RE-QUEST*, (Berkeley: University Of California, 1993).

9. Gary Cleveland, *Electronic Document Delivery: Converging Standards and Technologies,* UDT Series On Data Communication Technologies And Standards For Libraries, Report #2 (Ottawa: IFLA International Office For Universal Dataflow And Telecommunications, 1991).

10. CARL, *Discussion Paper: CARL Alliance Document Delivery Express,* (Denver: Colorado Alliance of Research Libraries, 1993).

11. Tony Barry, "Use Of E-Mail To Transmit Scanned Images Between Libraries," Electronic Message On Carl_l: Carl User's Information List, dated 24 Dec., 1993.

DOCUMENT DELIVERY IN THE 1990s : AN OVERVIEW

Lee Anne George
Librarian for Information and
Document Delivery Services
Harvard University

INTRODUCTION

Document delivery has become the hot topic of the 1990s. There has been a breathtaking increase in the number of document suppliers and in options for ordering and receiving documents. New information delivery systems are introduced so frequently that it is impossible to describe the range of new services in a limited number of pages. Rather than attempt the impossible, this essay will highlight some of the changes that have resulted in the current state-of-the-art of document delivery services and outline future developments.

DOCUMENT DELIVERY

The term "document delivery" is being used to describe a number of related, but different activities. A standard definition has yet to emerge. In this essay, the term defines the delivery of a copy of an article, report, or other document to a user. Unlike the traditional book loan, the user may keep the copy.

The state of document delivery follows developments in two parallel arenas: the method of scholarly communication and the automation of research tools and library processes.

Scholarly Communication

For the past 150 years the standard medium for the dissemination of scholarly output has been the printed journal. This medium grew out of the scholar's practice of recording notes, thoughts, observations, conversations, meetings, and letters in a personal diary, or journal. Compared with the time it takes to bring a book to print, the journal has been considered the fastest way to share research results with a wide audience. Nonetheless, with the necessary, but time-consuming, delays in the process of writing, peer-reviewing, editing, and rewriting scholarly articles, the information in scientific journals can hardly be called current.

The method of scholarly communication is gradually migrating from this paper-based medium to an electronic one. By using telephone, fax machine, electronic mail, electronic bulletin boards, and interactive electronic research notebooks, scholars can conduct, share, review, and edit their work in a more responsive and timely manner. Electronic communication has already made an impact on how scholarly information is delivered, stored, and retrieved. It will profoundly change information delivery in the future.

Automation of Research Tools and Library Processes

During the past twenty years, several waves of automation have dramatically affected how research is conducted and how information is retrieved. The first wave hit in the early 1970s, and the process of identifying relevant journal articles became easier as indexing, abstracting, and cataloging services were automated. Considerable resources were expended to develop better databases of journal literature and more powerful software for searching the databases. Researchers benefitted from the greatly enhanced ability to pinpoint citations to relevant articles precisely and quickly. Since the seventies were a time of healthy library budgets, the researcher could assume that most of the articles would be found in journals in the local library. If they were not, the real work began because access to resources outside the local library was limited. The process of locating libraries that owned the journals, placing orders, and awaiting delivery by mail was extremely low-tech and slow. The time required for an interlibrary loan transaction unquestionably impeded research efforts.

In a paper presented at the 2nd International Online Information Meeting in 1978, P. D. Gillespie described the need for an online document ordering and delivery system to support online database searching.[1] He quoted some estimates that indicated that a researcher needs, or has interest in, an article for about a week after it is identified. After that amount of time, the researcher moves on to a new area of interest. Gillespie detailed the study he was conducting to determine whether online searching had, or would have, an impact on document requests made by researchers. He discovered they did not even bother to fill out a request because they knew it would take interlibrary loan two or more weeks to receive the article. He concluded that researchers might be encouraged to order documents if they were likely to be delivered in a timely manner.

As the first automation wave was improving how quickly article citations could be identified, several successive waves addressed this need to improve the speed of transmitting requests for copies of articles. The following timeline highlights a few of the rapid advances in request transmission capabilities.

In the mid 1970s, TELEX was the "high-tech" method of sending document requests between libraries. This was a significant improvement over typing and mailing ILL forms because it eliminated the inherent mail delay.

In 1977 SDC (Systems Development Corp.) was the first, largest, and only commercial database host to offer an online document ordering service in the USA. The searcher would log into a parking file (Orbit), enter an account number, key in a citation, and identify one of the six possible document suppliers. The suppliers would periodically check their mail in the parking file, take out the orders, fill the order and mail the document to the requestor.

That same year CAN/OLE, the Canadian National Union Catalog Online Enquiry service, and CAN/DOC, a companion document ordering system, became available. These systems allowed researchers at 180 CAN/OLE centers to identify an article citation and to request a copy of the article in a single online search session.

In January of 1979, twelve libraries began testing the OCLC ILL subsystem. This system provided both electronic ILL request forms and electronic messaging between libraries. The messaging system allowed the requesting and supplying libraries to communicate about the status of requests.

In 1980, RLIN introduced its ILL Message File. This system also provided electronic ILL forms and messaging for status updates.

By 1987, the British Library Document Supply Centre (BLDSC) offered several Automated Request Transmission (ART) methods. Apparently, many BLDSC users were not ready for this automation wave— 65 percent of the document requests still arrived on typed forms through the mail.

Also in 1987, Engineering Information began accepting requests for articles indexed in Compendex Plus through DIALORDER and the STN system. This service permitted a researcher to order copies of articles from the Engineering Society Library as soon as she identified them through an online database search.

These and other similar developments accelerated the first portion of the document delivery cycle—identifying and requesting articles. Their success is driving the current wave of document delivery system automation advances.

CURRENT STATE OF DOCUMENT DELIVERY

Electronic Ordering Options

Paper request forms, such as the standard ALA ILL form, are still widely used and will continue to be used by some libraries. However, electronic ordering options are multiplying. Today, it is easy and commonplace to order documents from bibliographic database vendors after an online search has been completed. DIALOG, for example, lists more than forty vendors that offer this service.

Some CD-ROM products that are the equivalent of online databases let searchers upload document orders to suppliers electronically after searching the CD-ROM database. One example is the ROMULUS system produced by the National Library of Canada and the Canada Institute for Scientific and Technical Information (CISTI). ROMULUS allows a user to search four union lists of serials and then upload a request to one of three online ILL systems.

Electronic ordering via the ILL subsystems of the national bibliographic utilities such as OCLC and RLIN occurs every minute of every working day. Electronic orders can also be placed through a vendor's proprietary software, such as the British Library Document Supplier Centre's ARTel. Another option for some suppliers is to send requests via e-mail on the Internet.

Delivery Options

Regardless of the method by which the document was requested, it is still most often delivered in paper format. The speed with which it is delivered may be expedited by using express mail or overnight courier or fax, but the physical format has not changed. The second portion of the document delivery cycle—the actual delivery of the document from a remote location to the user—has only relatively recently experienced the same kind of automation developments as the first portion—identifying and requesting documents. Delivery of articles in electronic format has been technologically feasible ever since publishers began creating them electronically. Only recently has electronic delivery become common. Some publishers have been hesitant to make their publications available in an electronic format until questions about copyright and compensation are answered to their satisfaction. Other publishers have forged ahead with projects and services to discover just how electronic information will be used, to identify the user community, and to determine the types of electronic journals to make available.

Today, there are several options for retrieving the full text or full image of an article in electronic format that eliminate the step of "ordering" the document through interlibrary loan. First, the directory Fulltext Sources Online lists over 3600 online and CD-ROM titles that are available from sixteen vendors.[2] The vendor's search software takes the searcher directly to the article, which can be captured either electronically or in print. Second, via the Internet, searchers can find a document on a host computer and transfer it to their own computers where they can store, manipulate, or print it. Third, computers with fax modems and document scanning hardware, or
with scanners and file compression software such as ARIEL, make it possible to create and ship electronic documents between libraries or directly to patrons.

DOCUMENT SUPPLIERS

Currently, document suppliers run the gamut from those who have the article in a local collection to those who will go anywhere to get it for you. Here are six categories of document suppliers:

1. All types of libraries. So far, libraries still rely heavily on other libraries for copies of documents they can not supply from their own collections. Libraries supplement their collections through formal resource-sharing agreements within consortia, as well as through ad hoc arrangements with farflung libraries. They request documents from both traditional ILL operations and fee-based information services. An example of one of the largest library suppliers is the British Library Document Supply Centre.
2. Document clearinghouses. In addition to libraries, there are other suppliers that maintain large collections of documents and provide copies from their holdings. UMI's Article Clearinghouse and Dynamic Information are two well-known examples.
3. Database producer with their own collections. A number of database producers maintain collections of the documents used to create their bibliographic databases. Most provide document delivery to support online search-

ing of their databases. Some examples are ISI's The Genuine Article, Chemical Abstract's Document Delivery Service, American Mathematical Society's MathDOC, Engineering Information and Dialog's Article Express and Employee Benefits Infosource, to name a very few.

4. Tables-of-contents vendors. There are a growing number of databases that offer browsing of journals' tables of contents . The vendors all support their databases with document delivery, allowing browsers to order copies of articles while scanning the table of contents. Typically, the documents are supplied from libraries or other document collections. Two such vendors are UnCover/UnCover2 and Faxon Finder/Faxon Xpress.

5. Commercial information broker. These suppliers do not have collections of their own. Instead, they will track down documents regardless of their locations. One example of this category of document supplier is The Information Store.

6. CD-ROMS. Another type of document supplier brings whole collections of documents to researchers in a very compact form. Adonis and Broadcast News are examples of a growing selection of full-text, full-image, even full-motion documents on compact disc.

These are but highlights of the current variety of document suppliers. The electronic age promises new options for article-on-demand services.

WHAT DOES THE FUTURE HOLD?

Trend watchers predict a vast proliferation of electronic journals, newsletters, newspapers, and even audiovisual materials. Some believe that electronic publications will supplant paper ones. Others believe that, as with other technological advances, they will only supplement paper. In a paper published in the electronic journal The Public-Access Computer Systems Review in 1991, Ann Okerson, director of the Office of Scientific and Academic Publishing at the Association of Research Libraries, identified six categories of potential suppliers of electronic journals.[3]

1. Existing Publishers
Okerson foresees a future in which traditional publishers of scholarly information will make their products available in a variety of formats and packages. In this "parallel publication" model, some of the options will be paper journals, single article delivery, compendia of articles from several journals, publications-on-demand, parallel CD-ROM versions, and networked delivery to research facilities.
In this environment, subscription to information that is owned will be replaced by license to use the information for a certain period. Institutions may share multisite licenses for both paper and electronic publications. In the early days, the price of information may be higher than ever as new pricing structures are tested.

2. Intermediaries
   Okerson describes a number of organizations that have negotiated copyright agreements with publishers in order to deliver documents to their customers. These intermediaries include database producers, national document clearinghouses, all kinds of libraries, and "general" document suppliers. Okerson states, "the current pattern appears to be that publishers will assign rights in return for royalties to almost any reputable intermediary that makes a reasonable offer."[4]

3. Large Telecommunications Firms
   In 1991 there were only rumors about the regional phone companies' interest in bringing the information highway right into our homes. Recently, the press has been full of reports of battles between phone companies and cable companies for the right to replace the "last half mile" of copper cable with fiber optic cable. Today we read that a merger between two of the opponents was quietly taking place behind the scenes, and, that while the phone vs. cable battle raged, an electric company in Arkansas did the job itself.

4. Innovative Researchers and Scholars
   A number of computer-savvy researchers in a range of disciplines have bypassed the traditional publishing system and created their own electronic-only journals. In 1991, Okerson counted thirty networked electronic scholarly journals, eight of which were refereed or lightly refereed, and at least sixty electronic newsletters. The third edition of the Directory of Electronic Journals, Newsletters and Scholarly Discussion Lists, published by the Association of Research Libraries in April 1993, includes 240 electronic journals and newsletters. This upward trend is likely to continue.

5. University-based Electronic Publishing
   Okerson reported an estimate that universities currently publish less than 15 percent of their faculty's output. There has been much rhetoric about academia regaining control and distribution of its own intellectual output, and electronic publishing by universities is one way to achieve this. One example cited by Okerson is the Instant Math Preprints project. In a project that would include ten research universities, one university would host a database of preprint abstracts on its computer. The authors would deposit the full text of their preprints on their home institutions' computers. Users could search the abstract database and retrieve the complete preprint from the host computer via anonymous FTP (file transfer protocol.) Other preprint databases already exist.

6. Computer Conferences as Electronic Journals
   Researchers are using electronic bulletin boards and lists to test and discuss their ideas. Where once the journal was the unit of scholarly communication, and today the article is the relevant unit, in the not too distant future the idea may emerge as the truly important unit of communication between researchers. Electronic discussion lists are where this communication will take place.

CONCLUSION

These examples highlight trends in the rapidly changing world of document delivery that will forever change the ways resource sharing and interlibrary loan librarians supply research materials to users in an electronic environment. As additional document delivery options arise, librarians will have to decide which of several document formats to choose and whether to have them available locally or provide access to remotely stored ones. Librarians should consider the following points when making those choices:

1. Evaluate carefully the relative benefits of owning vs. licensing the information patrons need.
2. Determine what level of "connectivity" is appropriate and affordable. Libraries will need to get linked to the Internet if they do not want to be out of their patrons' information loop.
3. Stay informed about the ways patrons search for and use information. User behavior changes more slowly than technology. What is technically possible may not be acceptable to patrons.

REFERENCES

1. P.D. Gillespie, "Document Delivery for the On-line User -Near, Medium and Long-term Possibilities," Paper presented at 2nd International Online Information Meeting, 1978.

2. Fulltext Sources Online (Needham Heights, MA: BiblioData, 1993).

3. Ann Okerson, "The Electronic Journal: What, Whence and When?" *The Public-Access Computer Systems Review 2*, no.1 (1991): 5-24.

4. Okerson 14

31

ORDERING, DELIVERY AND TURNAROUND:
HOW DO DOCUMENT SUPPLIERS MAINTAIN THEIR MARKETS?

Mary A. Hollerich
Head of Interlibrary Loan and
Assistant Head of Access Services
University of Southern California

MARKETING 101

In a marketplace driven by competition, successful businesses provide goods and services that appeal to a particular segment of the consumer market, make their goods and services readily accessible to consumers, advertise and promote the product, and sell it at a price that compares favorably with the competition. Marketing theory sums up these goals in four simple concepts: product, place, promotion, and price.[1] These concepts comprise what is known as the marketing mix, a set of controllable variables that the company combines to create the desired response in its target market(s).[2]

The burgeoning document delivery marketplace is no different from any other industry in its application of these basic marketing principles. The commercial document delivery suppliers' product consists of both goods and services: subject collections, chronological holdings, and speed of processing, known as turnaround time, all tailored to meet the information needs of their target markets. Place refers to the delivery of documents to the requesters within an acceptable time frame. Promotion includes the methods used to create interest in their product, such as personal visits by sales representatives, exhibits at conferences, and catalogs. Finally, the price paid by consumers includes purchase fees for the documents, copyright royalties, database access, and special delivery charges.

According to McCarthy and Shapiro, target markets are formed by identifying consumers who have similar wants and/or needs and aggregating those consumers to form a relatively homogeneous market.[3] In today's information-based society, the target markets consist of end-users, who may be scholars or members of the general public, and intermediaries, such as reference and interlibrary loan librarians who are requesting on behalf of end-users. Aggregating these two market segments presents a challenge to document suppliers because end-users and intermediaries may have different levels of sophistication for searching and ordering documents, probably use different mechanisms for ordering and delivery, are willing to spend at different levels for the product, and very likely have different expectations for and definitions of turnaround time. In order to remain competitive with each other, document suppliers must be able to accommodate requests from both end-users and intermediaries. In fact, the document delivery supplier which most effectively meets the needs of its market gains a competitive edge in the rapidly evolving marketplace.

This essay will describe how commercial document delivery services apply the marketing concepts of product and place to fulfill the needs of, and therefore maintain, their target markets by: (1) making their collections readily accessible to users through a vast array of ordering options, from U.S. mail to the Internet and other electronic means; (2) utilizing a wide assortment of standard and expedited delivery options, allowing for considerable flexibility in speed and cost, and; (3) offering turnaround times that vary depending on users' needs and cost limitations, the document's date of publication, and the geographic location of the collection (e.g. in-house vs. remote collections).

DOCUMENT SUPPLIERS

Because of the proliferation of such services, not all suppliers can be included in this analysis. The suppliers discussed in this essay constitute a small portion of the document delivery industry, yet they represent all facets of the marketplace: (1) libraries that operate their own document delivery service, supplying materials from in-house collections; (2) document clearinghouses, similar to libraries but operating strictly on a for-profit basis; (3) database producers who provide an option for ordering documents cited in their bibliographic databases; (4) tables-of-contents vendors, similar to the database producers, but whose database coverage is title-based rather than subject-based; (5) commercial gophers who locate and retrieve documents wherever they might be available; and (6) full-text documents available on CD-ROM. The individual services under review include:

1. Libraries—British Library Document Supply Centre (BLDSC)
2. Document clearinghouses—Dynamic Information, UMI's Article Clearinghouse (UMI)
3. Database producers—Article Express, Chemical Abstracts Service Document Delivery Service (CAS), Employee Benefits Infosource, ISI's The Genuine Article (ISI), MathDoc
4. Tables-of-contents vendors—UnCover, Commercial gophers, Information Store
5. CD-ROM collections—Adonis, Broadcast News

The above commercial document suppliers will be used as examples of typical services available in the current marketplace and no attempt has been made to provide a comprehensive review of all service options available from each supplier. Due to the extremely dynamic nature of the document delivery industry, readers can contact suppliers directly with specific questions regarding current services and fees.

ORDERING OPTIONS

The "place" portion of marketing theory generally refers to the tactics an organization takes to deliver its product to targeted customers.[4] These steps are affected not only by the overall nature of the target market, but also by specific needs of smaller segments within each market. In the document delivery industry, ordering options are the primary means of making the document, or product, accessible to potential users, and the types of ordering options offered by each supplier depend upon the specific needs and wants of their markets and market segments.

The two primary market segments consist of end-users and intermediaries, who often have different needs for ordering. Intermediaries are more likely than end-users to be sophisticated database searchers, knowledgeable about system procedures and protocols, or even to be using complex databases and bibliographic utilities in the first place. The most frequently offered ordering options reflect the dual nature of the market segments: bibliographic databases and utilities typically used for traditional library functions such as reference and interlibrary loan, and the standard means of personal and scholarly communication, including mail, telephone, fax, and e-mail. As we will see, most of the suppliers reviewed in this essay target both end-users and intermediaries by offering numerous access methods in both categories.

Because libraries of all types (and therefore intermediaries) constitute a large portion of the document delivery market, some of the most widely available means of ordering documents are those heavily favored by reference and interlibrary loan librarians and online searchers: collections of databases, bibliographic utilities, and proprietary software designed specifically for this purpose.

Collections of databases, originally conceived as electronic bibliographic indexes, have been expanded within recent years to provide direct ordering of materials cited therein. Typical of such services are: Dialog, Orbit, BRS, and CAN (a collection of scientific and technical databases operated in North America by Chemical Abstracts Service, in Europe by FIZ Karlsruhe, and in Japan by JICST, ([the Japan Information Center of Science and Technology]).

Bibliographic utilities such as OCLC and RLIN also provide libraries and research centers with a large database of bibliographic citations and the option to order materials. Of these utilities, OCLC is by far the most widely offered by commercial document delivery services and is the primary utility for most interlibrary loan operations in the United States. Collections of databases and bibliographic utilities are attractive ordering options for intermediaries because they utilize existing equipment and network connections, and may not require additional training to use. A summary of ordering options via bibliographic databases and utilities is included in Table 5:1.

A number of propriety systems designed exclusively to facilitate document ordering are available from document suppliers such as UMI, BLDSC, and Article Express. These propriety systems permit document ordering by both intermediaries and end-users; however, the skill level, equipment and network connections required may in some cases preclude less sophisticated end-users from utilizing such services, while in other cases the systems might be viewed as archaic by those with state-of-the-art equipment.

UMInet provides end-users direct access to UMI via TYMNET telecommunications network. It provides clients with an electronic ordering and messaging system but requires users to submit citations in a structured, system-defined format. While the equipment requirements are rather low-end technology, more appealing to end-users, the system prompts do assume some familiarity with UMI's Article Clearinghouse holdings and catalog, suggesting that the target market is primarily intermediaries.

BLDSC offers two unique electronic ordering options, ARTTel and BLAISE. As with UMInet, ARTTel allows for file transfer or transmission of any number of citations; requests may be transmitted using any teletype compatible terminal and a modem linking it to a telecommunications line. Requests must adhere to a rigid format, and are then transferred to a minicomputer at BLDSC, where they are subsequently printed on forms and handled the same as postal orders. Because of its huge volume of overseas customers, many of whom reside in countries with underdeveloped telecommunications systems, BLDSC can provide end-users and intermediaries with the benefits of electronic transmission even if they don't have access to state-of-the-art equipment. BLDSC also accepts requests through BLAISE-LINE, the British Library's Automated Information Service, which has access to 21 databases including the major British Library catalogs and can be accessed via the Internet. BLAISE-LINE would best serve the needs of intermediaries and the more sophisticated end-users who are performing scholarly research and have Internet access.

Article Express, a joint venture between Dialog and Engineering Information, Inc. provides access to EI's collection of virtually all publications of the major engineering societies. Article Express also has developed its own ordering software, EiOrder, which permits users to capture orders for full-text documents electronically or enter them manually, then transfer the order by modem for immediate accessibility. EiOrder and installation instructions can be obtained at no charge by customers. Again, while this option might be intended to serve as a user-friendly access point for end-users, many may lack the sophistication and equipment necessary to utilize this option.

Tables-of-contents databases and CD-ROM collections of full-text/full-image articles are two examples of proprietary systems that meet the needs of intermediaries and novice end-users alike.

Tables-of-contents databases provide a convenient mechanism for both intermediaries and end-users to search and place orders for documents. UnCover is a prime example of such a vendor, and one that evolved as a result of marketplace competition. It originally accepted orders only through its UnCover database, and only for titles contained therein, limiting the potential market to those whose libraries purchased password and network access to UnCover. In a move to reach the broadest possible market and to extend their product line, however, UnCover recently began providing articles from volumes and even journal titles outside of its own collection using contracts with BLDSC and other research library collections. In addition, its UnCover S.O.S. service now permits flexible document ordering via fax, phone, e-mail and mail. These types of suppliers are especially attractive to end-users because they operate in the same familiar manner as a mail-order business where customers order directly and bill the charges to their credit cards.

The greatest advance in providing documents directly to the end-user comes from CD-ROM databases of full-text documents, such as Adonis and Broadcast News. With services such as these, the ordering option is really the search itself which yields the full text of the document immediately. Broadcast News is a collection of over 44,000 news items from a variety of radio and television news broadcasts. Adonis contains documents primarily in the biomedical disciplines. Installation of fulltext databases may prove more attractive than either other document delivery services or owning the materials themselves, because documents are instantly available and, in a networked environment, can be accessed by multiple users simultaneously. Because of the high cost of purchasing and maintaining subscriptions to CD-ROMs and the equipment required to store, view and print the documents, their market is currently limited to end-users and intermediaries whose libraries can afford them.

End-users represent the largest market growth potential and suppliers interested in the mass market are now offering those ordering mechanisms already used for personal and scholarly communication: phone, fax, mail, and e-mail. Even bibliographic utilities now offer user-friendly interfaces with document ordering options, such as OCLC FirstSearch. Table 5:2 provides an overview of ordering mechanisms using standard communications media.

Many suppliers, both large and small, offer ordering options through these communications media. Employee Benefits Infosource, whose collection comprises articles, books, reports and proceedings on all aspects of employee benefits, is an excellent example of how a very narrowly-focused subject supplier targets the endusers (very likely a larger market for them than academia) by accepting requests via phone, mail and fax. Chemical Abstracts' Document Delivery Service, providing journal articles, conference proceedings and symposia in chemistry as well as other scientific fields, accepts requests through phone, fax, mail and e-mail, in addition to several bibliographic databases and utilities, which enables them to reach both endusers and intermediaries.

Electronic mail is fast becoming the favored method of scholarly communication and, in an appeal to the research market, a growing number of document suppliers are accepting orders in this manner. Some suppliers have established e-mail addresses to which users submit orders just as they would any other e-mail message, while others have incorporated some method for electronic transfer of formatted bibliographic citations (the electronic equivalent of an order form). Still others have gone so far as to design their own software packages for requesting documents electronically.

Examples of suppliers that accept orders at their e-mail addresses include Dynamic Information and the American Mathematical Society's document delivery service, MathDoc. MathDoc's collection of mathematical journal articles and conference proceedings is readily accessible to both end-users and intermediaries through e-mail and Dialog.

Dynamic Information, which supplies materials from its own in-house collection as well as those of other institutions, permits its users to order any Dynamic Information document from their Internet e-mail address. In addition, they have teamed up with IEEE to provide access to a unique collection of engineering and computer science information, including the most comprehensive IEEE collection in the world. This service, called Ask*IEEE, also is available via Internet e-mail as well as Dialog. Like MathDoc, they successfully cater to both target markets through these order option channels, which is especially significant because many of the more sophisticated end-users who do their own document ordering are researchers in the scientific community.

Ordering options, however diverse they may be, represent only half of the process by which document suppliers make their products accessible and available to the target market; the other half of the process is the actual delivery of the completed order.

DELIVERY OPTIONS

While suppliers have enhanced the range of ordering options by quickly taking advantage of new technology, they have not been as quick to apply new technologies for electronic delivery. Instead, they continue to rely primarily on traditional paper-based systems. One possible explanation is that the required speed of delivery for any given order might be more closely related to the specific order or the individual requester's needs than to the needs or desires of the market as a whole. And since commercial suppliers are by nature profit-based enterprises, any investment in product development has to serve a significant portion of the market in order to make it financially worthwhile. Still, suppliers have incorporated a surprisingly large number of delivery options to meet the demands and cost limitations of the target markets as well as the smaller market segments.

Delivery options can be organized into three general categories: mail, overnight courier services, and electronic delivery, each of which has its own inherent advantages and disadvantages, and although some suppliers have developed unique methods for delivering a document, the available options tend to be much the same throughout the industry. Table 5:3 summarizes the delivery options offered by each of these suppliers at the time of publication.

Those document suppliers that provide a choice of delivery options include some form of mail delivery among their alternatives. The most commonly-used delivery method, mail services have the advantage of being relatively inexpensive and universally accessible, serving any market the supplier may be interested in reaching, regardless of geographic location. Typical forms include First Class and Express Mail for delivery within the United States and Air Mail for international shipment.

While readily accessible to both suppliers and consumers, the various forms of mail delivery are oftentimes too slow to satisfy clients who have grown accustomed to guaranteed overnight delivery for important business transactions or large academic institutions whose own mailing services compound the delay incurred by routine mail delivery. In an effort to accommodate these clients, many suppliers also offer expedited delivery via overnight couriers.

The most frequently used courier service in the document delivery industry is Federal Express, although Airborne Express, DHL and UPS are also rather commonly used. Because of the shippers' additional delivery fees, which can be substantial, document suppliers usually offer flexible billing: request delivery charges be billed to their own account with the shipper or be billed for such charges directly by the document supplier. Such flexible billing, which accommodates both intermediaries and end-users, demonstrates how document suppliers gain a competitive edge in the marketplace: clients perceive choice as being inherently good, and a supplier which offers many choices stands a greater chance for success.

The drawbacks to all these services, including overnight couriers, are that they add a significant amount of time to the process and are generally limited to delivery on weekdays during regular business hours, which may be acceptable for library staff who work those same hours, but not for end-users. Consequently, suppliers have incorporated electronic delivery alternatives to circumvent these delays: fax and Internet delivery and CD-ROM collections are the most commonly used.

FAX is the most universal medium for electronic delivery. It is used for routine business transactions, interlibrary loan delivery, and even personal communication. Some suppliers, most notably UnCover, rely exclusively on fax for delivery, while others offer fax as just one of many options. Still, fax has its own inherent disadvantages. Although suppliers offer fax delivery almost as universally as they do mail, there are telecommunications charges involved, which can be significant and many are passed on to the consumer. To further detract from its utility, the quality of fax reproduction is often poor, which can prove disastrous for end-users dependent upon photographs, diagrams or scientific notations.

ARIEL for Windows and ARIEL for DOS 2.0, the Research Libraries Group's Internet-based delivery software, are two of the most exciting developments in document delivery technology. ARIEL is used with commercially available personal computers (either DOS or Windows environments), scanners and laser printers to transmit and receive bit-mapped images of documents via Internet. The quality of reproduction is outstanding, and there often is no charge for ARIEL delivery. Despite its increasing popularity within the library market, it is not widely offered by document suppliers, probably because it requires expensive equipment and network connections, and it has not yet been adopted by end-users for much the same reason. At the time of this writing, only UMI, Dynamic Information and Article Express offered ARIEL as an alternative, but a number of other suppliers are considering it.

Article Express has developed its own Internet-based delivery package, XpressNet, which is similar to ARIEL. XpressNet is a combination of MS Windows software products that permit scanning, transmission, and printing of bit-mapped images of documents via the Internet. It also provides for on-screen viewing and browsing of scanned images. As is the case with ARIEL, XpressNet's equipment requirements may prove cost-prohibitive for end-users, limiting its market appeal to intermediaries who already have the necessary equipment or the budget to purchase it.

CD-ROM databases such as Adonis and Broadcast News offer the ultimate in rapid delivery to end-users. Installation of such services provides real "on-demand" delivery of their contents for those whose needs warrant having such collections in-house and whose budgets can accommodate the costs associated with real time delivery of full-text documents.

The range of ordering and delivery options presented thus far is illustrative of an industry that struggles to meet the needs of a diverse and increasingly demanding research community. Suppliers are also focusing on their own internal work flow to expedite the process further.

TURNAROUND TIME

One area in which market competition has had a profound impact is that of turnaround time, the period of time required for a document supplier to complete an order. As ordering and delivery options become more automated, document suppliers find themselves pressured to streamline their own internal processing to provide the fastest response time possible. Some suppliers have responded by providing fast overall delivery, while others have created a tiered system of different turnaround times, depending on the document's format, its publication date, the location of the item, and the client's ability to pay. End-users and intermediaries are demanding ever-greater turnaround time on a consistent basis, yet are reluctant to pay additional fees.

Most of the suppliers reviewed for this essay advertise turnaround times of two to three working days, on average. Upon closer examination, though, a few trends emerge. First and foremost is the benefit of electronic storage of the document requested; collections of full-text documents on CD-ROM permit immediate turnaround time, as the end-user's search generates a filled order. UnCover has received permission from some publishers to scan documents the first time that they are requested and then store them electronically; subsequent orders for these documents can then be filled almost instantly, usually within an hour.

Another trend that emerges is that suppliers can provide certain types of documents more quickly than others, usually depending on either the publication date or location of the item requested. Document clearinghouses such as UMI and ISI that hold long runs of journals sometimes advertise different rates of turnaround time depending on the publication date of the item requested. For example, both ISI and UMI advertise a lengthier turnaround time, generally three to four working days, for articles published more than five years prior to the date of the request. In contrast, both suppliers are able to offer faster delivery, usually one to two working days, for materials published within the past five years. A similar time differential is involved when a commercial gopher such as Dynamic Information has to go outside its own collection to fulfill an order.

Finally, it becomes clear upon inspection of the suppliers' fee structures that faster processing is usually accompanied by higher costs. If the standard processing time is not satisfactory to the requester, most suppliers offer the choice of rush service to speed up the process, but such services usually come at a very high price. For example, Hurd and Molyneux (1986) found that UMI was able to deliver documents in a timelier manner than conventional library sources, but that UMI's service is "accompanied by slightly higher costs."[5] Currie (1987) concluded that "[s]peed of delivery can be gained from commercial sources, but at great monetary cost."[6]

One of the most important criteria in selecting a document supplier, turnaround time also happens to be a measure given to widely divergent and often conflicting interpretations. A typical transaction involves two or even three parties, depending upon whether the end-user is requesting directly from the supplier or through an intermediary. Each party, unfortunately, views the process from a very different perspective and measures turnaround time differently.

39

From the supplier's perspective, turnaround time is measured from the day the request is received until the day the item is prepared for shipment or the requester is notified of their inability to fill the order. Intermediaries and end-users requesting directly from the supplier generally calculate turnaround time from the day they initiate the request with the supplier until the day they receive the filled order. End users tend to measure turnaround from the day they submit the request to the intermediary until the day they receive the document or are notified of its receipt

To compound the confusion, suppliers generally calculate turnaround time in terms of business days only, while intermediaries and end-users may count either business or calendar days. Depending upon the ordering and delivery methods used, this definition of turnaround could add days or even weeks to the claims made by suppliers.

These differing viewpoints account in part for the great discrepancies reported by the suppliers and their clients and could result in customer dissatisfaction. The few published reports by librarians support this contention and seem to indicate a certain level of dissatisfaction in this aspect of product service.

The University of Texas at Austin conducted a small internal study comparing costs and turnaround time of various library and commercial suppliers. Their results, published as part of SPEC Kit #184, show an average turnaround time, from order to receipt of document, of 13.51 days for libraries versus 17.35 days for vendors.[7]

Hurd and Molyneux reported the preliminary results of a study conducted at the University of Virginia in which documents were ordered from both conventional interlibrary loan sources and UMI Article Clearinghouse.[8] Paired requests, those items received from both UMI and conventional sources, demonstrated a mean turnaround time of 11.1 calendar days and 7.7 business days for UMI, as compared with 14.9 calendar and 10.4 business days for conventional sources. The study reinforces the concept that the borrower's measure of turnaround time is considerably greater than the supplier's.

Hurd and Molyneux's study is also interesting for its data on standard deviation of mean turnaround times. They suggest that consistency is a desirable characteristic for any document delivery supplier; therefore, the standard deviation of turnaround time can be used as a measure of consistency with less deviation implying a more consistent service. While the mean turnaround times for UMI were slightly better than those for conventional sources, the standard deviations for UMI were higher, implying a greater variation in results and hence a less consistent service overall. This deviation from advertised turnaround times could prove extremely frustrating for end-users, ultimately resulting in a loss of business for suppliers who are targeting this market.

A similar study was performed at Cornell's Mann Library, in which requests were sent to three different types of suppliers, including: (1) publication-specific suppliers such as ISI, Chemical Abstracts, and the Commonwealth Agricultural Bureau, (2) an information brokerage service, Information on Demand, and (3) traditional interlibrary loan sources. Currie's findings conclude that commercial suppliers provide more consistent service than traditional library sources, and that commercial gophers obtaining materials from remotely-held collections have the longest average turnaround time.

One possible explanation for user dissatisfaction in these studies is that, in many cases, requesters were using mail or courier services for ordering and delivery. It is also significant to note that all of these studies pre-date widespread use of the Internet for document ordering and delivery; the additional fees associated with fax service precluded its use as well. Although both Currie's and Hurd and Molyneux's studies imply that faster delivery usually translates into higher costs, commercial document delivery holds great promise for those target markets or individual clients who need primarily fast delivery and can afford to pay the corresponding costs. Those suppliers best able to meet users' needs for near-instantaneous turnaround time on a consistent basis and at a reasonable price, however, will undoubtedly achieve the greatest market success.

CONCLUSIONS

Document suppliers maintain their markets using the same marketing ploys as any other industry. Their product consists of diverse collections, fees, ordering mechanisms, delivery options, and turnaround times designed to meet the information needs of specific target markets and market segments. Those markets are comprised primarily of end-users or intermediaries, such as reference and interlibrary loan staff, ordering on behalf of end-users. Libraries that offer their users access to such suppliers, whether directly or through intermediaries, should consider the effects these services might have on staffing levels and classifications, equipment costs, copyright issues, and the library budget. Both library staff and end-users would serve their own interests best by remembering that commercial document delivery services are for-profit institutions and ought to be evaluated using the same market-savvy criteria that we use to evaluate any business and its product.

REFERENCE

1. E. Jerome McCarthy and Stanley J. Shapiro, *Basic Marketing*, 3rd Canadian ed. (Homewood, IL: Richard D. Irwin, Inc., 1983), 42.

2. Philip Kotler, *Principles of Marketing* 2d ed. (Englewood Cliffs, NJ: Prentice-Hall, Inc., 1983), 44.

3. McCarthy and Shapiro, *Basic Marketing*, 276.

4. Kotler 44.

5. Douglas F. Hurd and Robert Molyneux, "An Evaluation of Delivery Times and Costs of a Non-Library Document Delivery Service," *Energies for Transition: Proceedings of the Fourth National Conference* (Association of College and Research Libraries).

6. Jean Currie, "Document Delivery: A Study of Different Sources," *Quarterly Bulletin of the International Association of Agricultural Librarians and Documentalists* 32, no. 1 (1987): 16.

7. Tammy Nickelson Dearie and Virginia Steel, *Interlibrary Loan Trends: Making Access A Reality*, Association of Research Libraries SPEC Kit 184 (Washington, D.C.: Association of Research Libraries Office of Management Services, 1992) 103-106.

8. Hurd and Molyneux 182-183.

DOCUMENT DELIVERY:
THE CONFUSION OF IT ALL

Rosann Bazirjian
Assistant Director for
Technical Services
Florida State University

Pamela W. McLaughlin
Electronic Resources Coordinator
Syracuse University

INTRODUCTION

Today, when libraries are opening gateways to a multitude of electronic databases, they not only must decide among an array of services and information systems options, but also need to cope with many internal management decisions prompted by these new options. Planning for the adoption of these new services has an impact on library work flow on all levels, including reference service and interlibrary loan librarians, subject bibliographers, library administrators, library patrons. Certainly publishers and subscription agents are also challenged. Libraries are at a turning point in terms of ownership and access issues and are struggling over these obstacles in trying to find more efficient ways of delivering information. This essay focuses on the areas of confusion that the incorporation of document delivery services poses for many libraries, both conceptually and practically.

DEFINITION OF DOCUMENT DELIVERY

The phrase "document delivery" was first defined in 1983 by the Council of Library Resources as "the transfer of a document or a surrogate from a supplier, whether a library or document service, to a requesting library."[1] This definition recognized the distinction between traditional interlibrary loan (library to library) and document delivery (library/supplier to library). Yet, document delivery still means "different things to different people."[2] Today, document delivery is referred to as the provision of documents from a supplier to either a library or user. A further distinction is that the document, unlike an interlibrary loan book transaction, is not returnable. The user keeps the requested document.

PROLIFERATION OF AVAILABLE SERVICES

The proliferation of available document delivery services is confusing to those libraries that have decided to make a commitment and must now decide which service to choose. As both the number and scope of services continue to grow, it becomes increasingly difficult to keep up with current offerings. Libraries have to choose the best option to fill their users' needs. Often, the difficulty in selecting a document delivery service is that this is a relatively new service with, at this point, few available standards. Until the multitude of search options for filling requests is streamlined, libraries will be facing "an electronic tower of Babylon."[3]

In selecting document delivery services, the library must first decide whether to provide on-site or remote access to documents. This decision has serious financial implications, as on-site access comes with a considerably higher price tag than does remote access. Documents requested from remote services are priced by the unit, whereas, on-site access, an entire database of digitized images, has to be purchased.

Given the size of the database, contents, and special offers, the CARL UnCover Service, RLG's CitaDel and OCLC's ArticleFirst and ContentsFirst are examples of current leading electronic databases.

The UnCover Service is one of the largest on-line journal article sources. It currently contains over 4,000,000 articles from approximately 14,000 journals indexed back to 1989. UnCover provides keyword searching of names and article titles. The tables of contents (substantive articles, only) of journals are also covered. Once the user has selected the desired article, the user can place a request electronically, with the article's being faxed, usually within forty-eight hours. If the article has been scanned and stored on UnCover's optical storage device, the turnaround time may be as little as one hour or less. UnCover is available via the InterNet.

Pricing options for UnCover, however, are confusing. Libraries and users have a number of options from which to choose, all designed to provide flexibility in budgeting. For example, UnCover has an "Open Access" option, which allows anyone on the Internet to connect and order articles with a slightly higher service fee for those without accounts. Another option is to pay a subscription fee, which provides articles for a lower fee per article, currently $6.50. For high-volume users, a Standard or Customized gateway fee may be the preferred option. This provides a lower cost per article, customized screen, dedicated access, and annual bonuses of free articles. Local holdings can also be indicated for a fee per title. A deposit account is another option; with a deposit account, each article requested is deducted from the current balance of the account.

The CitaDel service was developed by the Research Libraries Group (RLG). A library can place a subscription for unlimited access to the databases. CitaDel provides document delivery of articles indexed in five commercial citation databases — Periodical Abstracts, Newspaper Abstracts, ABI/INFORM, Dissertation Abstracts, and Ei Page One, PAIS, —and four scholarly databases — Current Bibliography in the History of Technology, Index to Foreign Legal Periodicals, Index to Hispanic Legislation, and the Avery Index to Architectural Periodicals. Delivery is available via first class mail, fax, express courier, or RLG's ARIEL system. The fee for document delivery is currently $7.75 per article from the UMI/Data Courier files and $9.50 for the Engineering Index file.[4]

Inside Information, the British Library's new table-of-contents database, is available through CitaDel. It provides author, title, and journal citations to over 10,000 journals and magazines in the British Library Document Supply Centre, with coverage from October 1992 onward. Document delivery is available via CitaDel.

OCLC's ContentsFirst and ArticleFirst databases, accessible through OCLC's FirstSearch and EPIC services, contain over 11,000 journals representing a variety of disciplines, with coverage from 1990. ContentsFirst is a table-of-contents database that the user can search by journal title, subject, publisher, or ISSN number. Abstracts, if available, are also included in this database. ArticleFirst is a citation database that covers the same journals as ContentsFirst. "When something is ordered through FirstSearch, it is supplied by a vendor—in the current case—Faxon."[5] Delivery options include fax, overnight courier, or regular mail. A pricing package is available that allows a library to pay an annual fee for unlimited searching and for document delivery from the WorldCat, ArticleFirst, and ContentsFirst databases. One unique feature of FirstSearch is that, for libraries that use OCLC for cataloging, the system will inform the requester if the local library owns the title from which document delivery is being requested.[6]

In addition to these remote services, on-site access is another option. Examples of on-site services are ADONIS and UMI's Pro-Quest.

Adonis stands for Article Delivery Over Network Information Systems and is a full-text information source. A consortium of science publishers send their journals to the Adonis headquarters where they are then scanned, stored on CD-ROM, and made available to libraries by subscription. Approximately 500 medical titles are involved in this project. A library can order an article from ADONIS using a document delivery service such as UMI and Information on Demand or can view the article on an ADONIS workstation[7]. Copyright fees per article currently range from $3.50 to $7.00, depending on whether or not the library owns a paper subscription of the journal in which the requested article appears. In 1993, an annual subscription to ADONIS cost $16,000.[8]

UMI's ProQuest is an "image workstation,"[9] on which a user can search and print full-text articles from Business Periodicals Ondisc, General Periodicals Ondisc, Social Science Index, and IEE/IEEE Periodicals Ondisc. Once a desired article is retrieved, the user can request a copy of the article and have it displayed on the screen via the library's UMI IMAGEserver. This IMAGEserver receives the request, locates the article's image, and routes the article to a printer. The database is updated monthly and covers 1,000 titles back to 1988. Fax delivery is also an option. There are a multitude of other services available. Examples include the American Chemical Society's CAS Document Delivery Service, DOCLINE from the National Library of Medicine, ERIC Document Reproduction Service, National Technical Information Services, Engineering Index, and DIALORDER from Dialog. Suffice it to say, other services are available and are also vying for libraries' business.

EVALUATIVE CRITERIA

With all of these options available, on what criteria does a library make its decision as to how or whether to use a document delivery service? Performing both a needs assessment and cost-benefit analysis of services under consideration will enable libraries to make informed decisions. Done well, these activities represent a significant investment of time. Some criteria to consider include the following:

1. types of services available and their comparative costs
2. type of account desired
3. average turnaround time
4. fill rate
5. degree of difficulty in using the service (end-users and/or staff)
6. availability of Boolean searching
7. titles covered by the service, number and subjects
8. databases and retrospective holdings available
9. frequency of update
10. methods of delivery available
11. technical support

PROLIFERATION OF DELIVERY METHODS

Turning from the confusion that the proliferation of services causes, we should also consider the range of systems and means of access available. Here, fax is the predominant means of delivery of articles. However, U.S. Postal Service, United Parcel Service (UPS), Federal Express, courier service, express delivery options, such as UPS's Next Day Air or Second Day Air, are also common delivery options. Many libraries will opt for different delivery methods, depending on their budget and needs.

In addition to these more traditional means of access, electronic delivery is becoming an option. In 1992, 3,000 journals and newsletters were available on-line.[10] Information Access Corporation is one leader in this area, with over 1,000 titles available in full-text in their databases.

The Research Libraries Group's ARIEL is an electronic delivery system that combines direct copy scanning with Internet transmission. The supplier scans a document and transmits the image over the Internet. This process eliminates the need to photocopy the desired article, and hence makes the transaction more cost effective.[11] It also allows the supplier to store the image so that it can quickly be retrieved should a request for the same article be received in the future. ARIEL provides high-resolution images and is especially useful for all types of graphics.

Another means of delivery is the North Carolina State University/ National Agricultural Library's Digital Text Transmission Project. This MacIntosh-based hypercard application processes scanned images, as well as provides an option to download or transmit the article to a patron's workstation.[12] The uniqueness of this project is that it delivers articles directly to the user's desktop rather than through a gateway located in the library, thus offering direct delivery to an individual user.

An "Internet-fax gateway," by the Ohio State University Network Fax Project, is yet another delivery option. This project also utilizes the Internet, but combines Group III fax machines to transmit journal articles over the Internet to personal computers.[13]

Thus, with so many current electronic access and delivery options available and with more coming on market, the confusion yet grows. A library must decide upon a delivery method, be it fax or another delivery option. ARIEL is currently the only delivery method commercially available, primarily because it is economical and is used by numerous libraries and government agencies.

CONFUSED CONSTITUENCIES

The confusion caused by the proliferation of document delivery services and systems is exacerbated by the confusion among various constituencies, including subject bibliographers, public service staff, library administrators, patrons, publishers, and vendors.

Subject Bibliographers

As budgets shrink, exchange rates remain unfavorable, inflation continues to spiral upward, and universities downsize, subject specialist librarians are struggling over how to best build library collections and support service programs. Coupled with libraries' fiscal constraints is the volume of publishing, which continues to grow. For example, output in the field of physics has doubled in the last ten years.[14] In addition, patrons have greatly expanded access to information, available through the online systems and services developed and offered through libraries. Patrons' expectations for better and faster delivery services have certainly risen. Thus, bibliographers are facing the challenge of how better access when library budgets are tight. Today's decisions about information access require periodic review and rethinking in order to keep pace with the increase of information demands.

It is no longer the library within which information is physically stored. The library has moved from a "library of record" to a "library as the gateway to information."[15] It is all well and good to realize and understand that libraries are now in a world of access, coupled with ownership, and that libraries can no longer collect comprehensively, yet, on a day-to-day basis, librarians have some very challenging issues to address. One is the strong need for a more effective mechanism to coordinate collection development with resource sharing activities. Because of economic changes, more libraries are forging partnerships with other libraries within their region, analyzing subject collection strengths and weaknesses, and agreeing to establish reciprocal delivery agreements. For example, the Science and Technology Library at Syracuse University has such an agreement whereby science libraries in the Central New York region fax articles to one another free of charge.

Other concerns are the amount of budget that should be allocated to document delivery and the choice of journals to cancel in favor of on-demand access. These choices depend on the subject area for which the bibliographer is responsible. For example, subject selectors in the humanities may not need to divert as large a portion of their funds to access because their journals are relatively inexpensive, and many are not yet available electronically. Their counterparts may choose just the opposite. Since 1988, bibliographers at Syracuse University have consistently been asked to cancel their periodical and serial subscriptions in order to keep within declining budgets. In disciplines such as the sciences, cancellations have been especially heavy. Syracuse University Library established a line within the acquisitions budget for document delivery in 1992, diverting a portion of the traditional budget allocation to access rather than ownership.

47

Because many document delivery services only provide access to journals published within the last five years, the bibliographer also needs to decide whether backruns should be stored or discarded. Many bibliographers see the value in maintaining complete runs of titles, something not possible if libraries use document delivery suppliers. In short, bibliographers need to answer the question of how document delivery can complement their work, rather than complicate it. As Patricia Sabosik says, it is important that bibliographers begin to look at their collections of journals not as volumes, but "as an inventory of thousands of individual articles that they broker to a diverse user community."[16]

Public Service Staff

Those on the front lines charged with interpreting policies and explaining services to patrons have a particularly difficult task coping with these new document delivery services. How are electronic delivery systems, commercial information services, or library resource sharing networks? How, why, and who should be charged? How are individuals and/or departments billed? These are examples of confusing issues for public service staff. The ability to articulate clearly library policies and services is essential in making right decisions, and it requires thorough study, planning, and communication among those areas affected.

Library Administrators

Administrators are ultimately responsible for the decisions related to document delivery. The political ramifications of embracing document delivery are of particular concern to this group, including target audience, costs and charge-backs, and infrastructure issues. To whom document delivery services are to be offered is often easier to decide than which services to select. The target audience for such services is typically the same as that of interlibrary loan — faculty, staff, and students. Restricting service is difficult to justify, yet it may be too costly to offer subsidized document delivery to a larger clientele. Where to deploy service is also an important question. Reference may be a more logical service point since users are accustomed to seeking assistance here. Interlibrary loan is a possible service point since document delivery may be viewed as an extension of ILL activities. In some universities, acquisitions or serials departments present an attractive option, with staff already trained in acquiring material and familiar with journal publishing. They are also familiar with vendors and payment processing, though are distant from direct contact with users. When more and more research materials are delivered directly to the user's desktop computer, deployment for this particular service point may not be essential in the future. As serial subscriptions continue to decline, ILL and document delivery are fulfill more of the need for research materials.

At the same time, administrators are facing many fiscal issues. How will libraries subsidize the service? Under what circumstances should the patron pay? For example, should the patron pay for a loaned item because the library's copy was mutilated or vandalized? Should patrons or libraries pay for rush requests? Can ILL provide a fast turnaround time? Because of the great variety of document delivery services available, determining a pricing structure and subsidy can be quite complicated.[17] Also, administrators must determine how funds should be established and allocated to subsidize ILL's use document delivery.

Library Patrons

In today's information environment, it is difficult for patrons to be aware of all current service offerings, to keep up with changes in each offering, and to know if they are eligible to access these services. Do they have the proper affiliation? Whom do they ask for help or interpretation? What category of material may be requested from document delivery? which titles they order? Titles that the library does not own, or articles from journals that have been misplaced, vandalized, sent to at the bindery, etc.? Can they only request a title if it is needed rush? What is the library's definition of rush?

Publishers

Many publishers are experiencing different concerns as they realize the pressure of user preference for electronic access to journals. Of prime concerns are copyright issues. Copyright fees for electronic delivery vary greatly from publisher to publisher and the basis on which fees have been established is seldom clear to those using these services. lower fees may be viewed as encouraging document delivery and higher fees discouraging it, which is not necessarily the outcome desired by publishers. Furthermore, publishers are concerned about their loss of control of presentation and quality of their product in the electronic age. This loss of identifiable intellectual property is perceived as threatening to publishers. With print formats, publishers appear to have complete control of the content and layout of their publications. When texts are transmitted digitally, the publishers may lose the control over these areas.

Publishers are already challenged by the uncertainty of technological advances altering traditional production techniques. Do they begin to explore electronic options or merely continue business as usual? When financial success depends on this decision, publishers must make it their prime focus. After all, their bottom line is at stake.

Library Vendors

Vendors have traditionally been secure in the role they played for libraries. Services from vendors includes providing materials promptly with consolidated invoices and statistical reports relating library budget expenditures and converting currency on invoices. Now, that sense of security is receding. As vendors try to "develop products and services to match librarians' changing expectations,"[18] vendors are facing a shift from their old role and being forced to reevaluate their services, especially as libraries continue to cancel journal subscriptions and downsize collections. In order to survive, vendors need to look at alternatives, such as document delivery. Vendors need to accept a whole new group of clientele, simply because purchasing decisions are broadened. Decisions can be made by the acquisitions librarian, serials librarian, reference librarian, access services librarian, library liaison, subject specialist, interlibrary loan librarian, or any combination of these people.

CONCLUSION

Confusion abounds as libraries embark on a future of digital delivery to complement ownership. This is not an entirely new issue, but one that is becoming more complicated as questions with no easy answers are posed. It is clear that librarians are not faced with just one or two choices, but with a proliferation of services and systems that may be overwhelming to librarians. With so many distinctions to be made, a solid understanding of the significant differences is extremely difficult to develop, yet essential to decision-making. The ground is shifting under their feet, and administrators and librarians are facing the questions of how to arrange work flow to accommodate new services, how to subsidize or charge for using document delivery services, and how to promote these services to patrons. In this ever-changing environment, new technologies have changed the old roles and rules in libraries and have generated much confusion.

REFERENCES

1. Anne McGee, "Article Delivery: Shifting Paradigms," *Serials Librarian* 23, nos.3/4, 1993:209.

2. Lee Anne George, "Fee-Based Information Services and Document Delivery," *Wilson Library Bulletin* 67, no.6, 1993:41.

3. Ronald G. Leach, and Judith E. Tribble, "Electronic Document Delivery: New Options for Libraries," *The Journal of Academic Librarianship* 18, no.6, 1993:364.

4. Michael Rogers, "Research Libraries Group Debuts CitaDel on RLIN," *Library Journal* 117, no.10, 1992:36.

5. Pat Ensor, "Automating Document Delivery: A Conference Report," *Computers in Libraries* 12, no.11, 1992:36.

6. Kathy M. Jackson, and Nancy L. Buchanan, "Unlimited Access to FirstSearch: an *Online* Success Story," Online 17, no.5, 1993:42.

7. Julie Wessling, "Document Delivery: A Primary Service for the Nineties," *Advances in Librarianship* 16, 1992:17.

8. Leach 362.

9. Wessling 17.

10. Georgia Finnigan, "Document Delivery Gets Personal," *Online* 16, no.3, 1992:107.

11. Wessling 7.

12. Wessling 10.

13. Mary E. Jackson, "Document Delivery Over the Internet," Online 17, no.2, 1993:20.

14. Leach 360.

15. Peggy Johnson, "When Pigs Fly, or When Access Equals Ownership," *Technicalities* 12, no.2, 1992:6.

16. Patricia E. Sabosik, "Document Delivery Services: Today's Electronic Scriptoria," *Computers in Libraries* 12, no.11, 1992:17).

17. Finnigan 108.

18. John Cox, "Changing Role of the Subscription Agent, " *Interlending and Document Supply* 2, no.3, 1992:109.

TOTAL QUALITY MANAGEMENT FOR
INTERLIBRARY LOAN AND DOCUMENT DELIVERY

Amy Chang
Head of Access Services
Texas Tech University

INTRODUCTION

In today's high-tech environment, technological advances have not only accelerated information access, but have created new demands for information service. As users explore information sources available worldwide, the buying power of libraries is decreasing and the cost of research materials continues to mount. This economic climate has altered the traditional concept of building strong local collections and supplying research materials. As a result, new demands for information needs have yielded greater opportunities for interlibrary loan (ILL) and document delivery service. More than ever before, libraries are dependent on online networks, resource sharing agreements, and electronic information services to satisfy the research needs of their clientele.

ILL and document delivery librarians are challenged by technological and economic changes. In order to have a role in tomorrow's information delivery, libraries must adopt Total Quality Management (TQM) as a way to reconceptualize service, rethink service operations, and reengineer complex work processes. This means that TQM must be defined, implementation strategies planned, and outcomes evaluated and reevaluated on an on-going basis so that research materials can be delivered to library users in the most cost-effective and timely manner possible.

CHALLENGES AND ISSUES FOR ILL AND DOCUMENT DELIVERY

In the 1990s, the concept of TQM has become an effective management strategy in both the private and public sector. The primary goal of TQM, in the business sector, is to meet customer needs, wants, and desires. The emphasis is on continuous improvement that ensures the development of quality products and services. This focus, shifted from organization-driven to customer-driven, has revolutionized work processes in various service-oriented businesses and it has resulted in increased productivity and reduced costs. As Lloyd Dobynes and Clare Crawford-Mason state, "We're talking about quality as a better way of producing goods and services, a way that eliminates waste, gives employees pride in their work, and keeps the customer coming back for more."[1]

Before the electronic age, paper indexes and card catalogs were the primary tools library users needed to locate research materials. To access a broad range of research information, patrons spent an enormous amount of time and effort using these tools manually and sequentially. When telecommunication networks were not available and accessing other sources was not an option, researchers had to depend on physical access to the local collection. ILL filled gaps in the local collections. Weeks could be spent on verifying the title, processing the request, and waiting for the arrival of the material When charges occurred, patrons had to absorb loan charges.

However, a vision of TQM for ILL and document delivery has emerged in the early 1990s. The traditional ILL services have been challenged by three forces: commercial information services, information users, and changes in technology and economics.

Commercial information services

Information systems have empowered users with a wide array of databases. By entering a keyword or a string of keywords, the computer instantly pulls, sorts, and displays relevant titles and citations, many of which are accompanied by abstracts. Services, such as UnCover, FirstSearch, DIALOG, CAS, RLG, offer a "just-in-time" document delivery service directly to users. With these new and prompt information delivery services on the market, the traditional ILL process that may take days is no longer acceptable to users. Users' expectations for rapid processing and quick delivery service force libraries to develop new ideas and methods for implementing speedy delivery services.

Information users

When bibliographic records, citations of articles, and even full texts of articles can be retrieved by the movement of fingertips, library users will expect ILL to be equally convenient, responsive, and prompt.

Users' expectations lay a new ground for challenging the traditional ILL process. Nevertheless, this challenge has yet to be accepted by many librarians. Barbara B. Higginbotham states that, "The added speed offered by telecommunication and computers has not changed the approach of some library professionals who continue to believe that there is no great need for haste, and that patient readers will be grateful for the document, whenever it arrives. Staff seemed reluctant to raise the expectations of students and faculty, whom they had so carefully trained over time to wait."[2]

However, information users in the fast-paced electronic age demand more because they have more and better options in accessing research information and material that enable them to compare the quality of the services offered. With new options on the market, users who are dissatisfied with the ILL service will choose electronic tools or commercial document delivery services rather than ILL. In competing with commercial information services, librarians need to be aware that power has passed to the consumer. "More competition, more choices, put more power in the hands of the customer, and that, of course, drives the need for quality."[3]

To survive in tomorrow's information society, libraries must take users' needs into serious account. John V. Lombardi, President of the University of Florida, stresses that "We have to recognize students as significant people whose needs, comfort, and success take high priority within the institution. If we choose faculty comfort, administrative convenience, and management ease over student satisfaction and success, we deserve to lose the war."[4] Although his statement urges faculty and university administrators to prioritize students' needs, it is also relevant to libraries' responsibility to their clienteles and the consequence we might face if we choose otherwise.

Changes in Technology And Economics

Most library budgets have not been able to keep up with the high inflationary rate in library materials. If additional money has been available, it is usually used to offset inflation. Also, the space to house library materials is more costly than ever. Libraries no longer have spare dollars to collect and store "just-in-case" materials. Meanwhile, electronic databases gather gigantic amounts of information, using the information super highway to transmit information at high speeds. As more users are connected to information databases, information access is no longer localized; it becomes globalized.

More than a decade ago, N. John Naisbitt in Megatrends stated that 6,000 to 7,000 scientific articles were written each day[5]. The number of scholarly journals has risen from 70,000 to 108,590 in twenty years[6]. Naisbitt pointed out that "In the computer age, we are dealing with conceptual space connected by electronics rather than physical space connected by the motorcar."[7] This conceptual space has transformed the traditional library into a virtual library in which users are electronically linked directly to information. The size of the library's location collection was once the primary measure for satisfying users' needs. Now, the local collection serves as just another option as patrons gather research materials.

To be competitive in tomorrow's information world, today's ILL service must be responsive to the forces of these changes. This means that delivery systems must be linked with telecommunication networks and users' needs must be filled by expedited resource sharing that utilizes both consortia resource sharing networks and access to commercial information services.

TQM DIMENSIONS FOR ILL AND DOCUMENT DELIVERY

TQM dimensions for ILL and document delivery involve three basic, interconnected components: service, technology, and management. Quality service is dependent on the utilization of new technology and the effectiveness of resource management. Ever-changing information systems have an impact on every aspect of today's and tomorrow's document delivery service, and as a result, TQM becomes a dynamic means of attaining quality productivity/service. (See Figure 6.1)

Service

Due to technological changes, information access has expanded from library-to-library service to resource sharing networks, global information access, and electronic document service. Many libraries have transformed the traditional ILL into

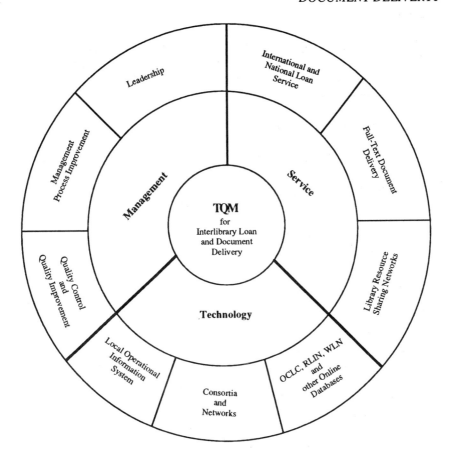

Figure 6.1 TQM for ILL and document delivery

document delivery to include such services as campus delivery, courier service, re-source sharing agreements among libraries, and subsidized commercial document delivery.

To be competitive in tomorrow's technological environment, today's libraries must continue to seek innovative ways to satisfy information users' new demands and to envision services that are differentiated from commercial information services in order to permit users to continue to rely on library's sources and services. Doing so, TQM services must be achieved, service visibility must be increased in the community, and out-reach programs must be planned.

In this changing process, ILL librarians need not only to possess skills and knowledge to conduct advanced searches and to navigate among a diversity of electronic databases, but also to evaluate continuously the outcome of the delivery system so that a differentiated and more sophisticated information delivery system can be developed today and ready tomorrow.

Technology

New options for information delivery service involve computerized delivery systems such as e-mail, FAX, and ARIEL transmission, electronic delivery systems connected to personal computers or workstations, and electronic journals, newsletters, and bulletins. The power of information systems has offered many more alternatives to ILL; more importantly, it imposed new roles on the ILL and document delivery librarians. These new roles include

1. Identifying the emerging information technologies that are likely to have an impact on information access and services;
2. Foreseeing the changes in information delivery systems;
3. Managing risks for adopting new information technologies for operating ILL and delivery services; and
4. Articulating the need for restructuring the organization in order to respond to new patterns of work caused by new technology.

Although information and materials are delivered to users in much less time than in pre-electronic times, tasks for processing requests, complying with copyright, maintaining files, and retrieving records are still labor-intensive. In order to meet the demand for prompt service, the slow manual process of handling these tasks must be streamlined and computerized to allow ILL operations to compete with commercial delivery service. For example, an in-house information database can be developed to convert ILL data from online systems, such as OCLC, to generate copyright and statistical reports, retrieve records, and compile operational and management information.[8]

Today's ILL librarians need to know how to use technology not only to make old processes work faster but "to break old rules and create new ways of working."[9]

Management

ILL and document delivery activities are complex. They involve managing policies, procedures, codes, agreements, and copyright. In meeting the demands for timely information delivery in the electronic age, ILL staff must not focus excessively on these procedures and thus forget how customers are served. Rigid procedures for borrowing and lending materials must be re-engineered, and work processes must be managed in a most cost effective way. This change must provide the flexibility to allow a quick shift in work processes to adjust to new economic situations or technological advances. Moreover, staff must be trained to spend more time doing real work that directly serves users' needs and less time in manual procedures—such as filing tasks, compiling statistics, and generating copyright reports. They should continuously evaluate and re-evaluate any task that slows down the process of obtaining loan materials. Additionally, quality control and quality improvement must be integrated into the work processes to reduce service cycle time (turnaround time) and to be cost-effectiveness. Doing so, managers need to oversee ILL and document delivery operations through service perspectives and must be able to

1. Allocate and mobilize resources, optimizing tangible and intangible elements;
2. Analyze work flow to maximize productivity;
3. Manage for technological changes, including training staff to develop new skills;
4. Adapt to information technology and new delivery systems in order to obtain timely information for users; and
5. Minimize costs.

IMPLEMENTATION STRATEGIES FOR TQM

TQM will not be adopted in a library if managers and staff fear that service improvements will increase service demands. The conventional analogy of a trade-off between quality and cost forces managers to focus on operational savings, rather than on improving the quality of service. This approach loses sight of users' needs and overlooks the commercial document delivery options. When saving money causes a decrease in service quality or service options, users will look to commercial information brokers for better service. Consequently, the role of libraries in supplying information may be diminished.

To overcome the financial constraints under which most librarians work, today's ILL and document delivery librarians need to understand new cost management concepts in order to optimize resources. When costs are minimized and demands for service continue to increase, the top library administrators must provide the financial support for staffing and equipment to sustain total quality service and productivity.

Managing Costs

Modern cost management is the process of understanding operational processes and service delivery, not just a money-saving action. It assists managers in tracking and analyzing expenditures with the objective of eliminating, reducing, or containing costs associated with operations, while emphasizing customer/user satisfaction. This process enables managers to discern cost factors in order to optimize tangible resources (equipment and facilities) and emphasize intangibles (reliability, responsiveness, assurance, and empathy) that foster a good work ethic among staff.[10]

Managers need to be aware that TQM does not automatically result in more equipment, more staff, and better materials. Managers should grasp budget constraints as an opportunity to reevaluate operational processes with a goal of reducing or eliminating labor-intensive tasks or redundancies or duplicated effort.

Poor service and low productivity are produced by inadequate equipment and outmoded methods, which can cost the library even more to maintain than to improve. As David A. Garvin states, "what is needed is a revolution in the way managers think about the continuum of [service] development activities. By this we do not mean a shift only in their conventional approaches to quality problems but also in their readiness to make the long-term investments in people and equipment necessary to make better [service] less expensive."[11] Quality productivity can be achieved when equipment and new technology are wisely invested and innovation and creativity are encouraged.

Figure 6.2 illustrates how resources can be maximized for achieving TQM and differentiates the TQM from the traditional service approach to controlling cost:

	Traditional Cost Control	TQM Cost Management
Service	Suppressing service demands. Maintaining minimum or current service level.	Analyzing service demands. Enhancing, emphasizing, and enlarging service. Developing new service perspective.
Costs	Using service/costs "trade-off" to justify costs. Requiring high investment for staffing and equipment in achieving quality service. Eliminating services to achieve cost control.	Analyzing intangible and tangible factors. Leveraging value over costs. Optimizing resources. Long-term investment in people and new technology to make better service less expensive.
Management	Using inadequate equipment, low work performance, and outmoded methods. Perceiving change altering the stable environment and resisting change. Managing work load with rigid job description.	Developing new skills and knowledge. Working on service values, goals, and vision. Utilizing people's talents and expertise, and sustaining innovation. Investing in equipment and new technology Prioritizing quality service/productivity.

Fig.6.2. Comparison of traditional approaches to cost control with TQM approach

Managing Human Resource

Reevaluating operational processes for TQM cost management can lead to change. According to Garvin's quality service study, there are many inevitable disruptions within the organization when dealing with change. Additional efforts will be needed to establish new operations, processes, and skills. The immediate impact of these efforts is likely to result in a reduction in productivity in the short term. New ways of operating are seldom absorbed immediately. Learning and adjusting to new procedures normally requires an up-front investment of time and energy. The transition can be disruptive.

In order for change to be introduced successfully, goals must be institutionalized by library administrators, who must openly advocate high-quality productivity, reinforce the value of service as a long-term goal for the library, and improve the organizational culture. The leadership will allow middle managers to take action. This process requires emphasizing job satisfaction, developing quality training programs, establishing quality measurements/standards, and organizing team management.

Emphasizing Job Satisfaction. The emphasis on job satisfaction should lead people to perceive change as an opportunity to improve job performance, rather than as a threat to job security. Any change that will affect personnel positions and work groups should be communicated before the change is made. Creating challenging and rewarding activities can minimize the resistance. The manager should share information to enable staff to internalize the value of their productivity and contributions in the process.

Developing Quality Training Programs. Staff will need to improve skills and gain new expertise in this ever-changing technological environment. Staff should be encouraged to use creativity and autonomy to accomplish their jobs. Through a TQM training program, staff will understand not only how to perform the job right, but also why they are doing the job. This new learning experience should improve on-the-spot problem solving and minimize errors in work procedures.

Establishing Quality Measurements/Standards. Systematic measures of service and work performance should be established to encourage staff to achieve consistency in producing quality service. Standards must be established for improving turnaround time, increasing filling rate, minimizing operational costs, and targeting zero-error. High performance staff should be acknowledged and rewarded. Managers should recognize that fulfilling an individual's needs for prestige and recognition is a major responsibility.

Organizing Team Management. Teamwork means that members share information, learn skills from one another, solve problems together, and share the excitement of productivity and quality work that the team produces. Employees' commitment plays an important role in fostering a quality culture in the organization, as their decisions are instrumental in determining how quickly plans can be implemented with minimal mistakes[12].

Managers at all levels should support creativity and innovation and direct positive change in work behavior. They must use management strategies to identify barriers to change, diagnose problems, and generate alternatives for achieving TQM.

Outcome Assessment

Outcome assessment consists of internal and external analyses. It evaluates facts and data, and thus ensures the effectiveness of TQM.

"Those years when organizations could afford capital and time to correct wrong management practices are over." Jessica Keyes states, "Today's economic weather is clearly much darker and more stormy. There are no spare dollars to throw around."[13] Facing this unstable economic situation, outcome assessment becomes a vital key for effective planning and decision-making. It is heavily dependent on collecting indicators and data and on the conversion of that data into useful management information.

Outcome assessment involves two aspects: (1) Internal environment analysis takes serious account of organizational capabilities and is directed to the exploitation of strengths in order to avoid weaknesses. Elements of internal analysis include finances, human resources, management, and equipment. The auditing process provides an opportunity to analyze strengths, uniqueness, and weaknesses of the organization. (2) External environment analysis assists in determining targeted and potential audiences, articulating the impact of new technology on information service, and studying changes in the use of information.

Overall, the strengths of ILL and document delivery operations are the use of new technologies that connect libraries to other sources (e.g., electronic databases, various commercial document delivery services), competent employees willing to adapt to technological and economic changes to offer more to users utilizing fewer resources, and library users who believe that their needs can be satisfied by libraries. The weaknesses are associated costs, preoccupation with internal processes, and relative slowness.

Today's computers do more than simply automate work processes: computers can transform operational data to useful information to allow managers to evaluate service activities and productivity. For example, a local ILL information system that downloads records from OCLC or local resource sharing networks can generate reports to monitor user's status and material borrowed. It becomes possible to relate service demands to user's and to view gaps in the collection. Furthermore, computers can capture data on turnaround time and fill rates to measure current performance against a quality standard. Using in-house outcome assessment wisely, managers will be able to evaluate, improve, and design services effectively and improve service on an ongoing basis.

Process-Driven

Recently, a new process-driven paradigm has evolved from the function-driven management style. A "function-based" organization is based on discrete tasks being passed from one employee or unit to the next. These steps not only slowdown the process, but also add costs. The "process-driven" concept focuses on how services can be developed and delivered efficiently, rather than divided among individual workers. According to John A. Byrne's report, the process-driven concept is part of the reengineering movement that creates mobility within the organization, rather than confines the work process to individual job descriptions.[14] To apply the process-driven concept to ILL and document delivery operations, every employee in the department understands the function and operation of the service and is able to serve patron inquiries, to process requests and materials, to search items in online databases, and to work with ILL and document delivery systems and other electronic databases. To apply the process-driven concept to ILL and document delivery operations requires well-organized training programs, as well as staff opportunities to learn new skills and to use creativity and talents to produce quality work.

A level of staffing based on peaks in activity can no longer be supported by libraries. The process-driven approach, however, provides mobility within the department. An advantage of a local ILL information system is that it can be used to summarize operational data into descriptive work patterns (e.g., peaks, valleys, and distributions of productivity and delivery of services). Using this information, managers are able to determine fluctuations of work flow and to assign staff at adequate levels.

Marketing

Integrating the modern marketing concept to ILL and document delivery will do two things: first, it will anchor users' interests to library service; second, it will give the library an opportunity to review the research needs in the community, to realign service to user needs.

Rather than the conventional marketing approach of promotion and advertisement, modern marketing supports coordination of service demands and activities. Modern marketing involves the following processes:

1. Market analysis. Information users have diverse demands and desires. Librarians need to understand users' needs by segments and by individuals. Market analysis needs to identify current and potential users and to develop services for targeted groups.

2. Service position/promotion. As information industries aggressively offer quick and cost-effective information and document delivery services, libraries find they are competing with these new offerings. Today's ILL must not only be enlarged, enhanced, and emphasized, but opened to new markets in order to increase service visibility and create new dimensions for service.

3. Service differentiation. When more users connect to electronic databases, more information and research materials will be delivered directly to users. However, online full-text delivery or commercial delivery does not always fulfill research and scholarly needs. Today's administrators and librarians must ask themselves: What are these needs? How can the library fill these needs efficiently and effectively? How can the library be differentiated from services offered by commercial suppliers?

4. Quality control. Service cannot be promoted and will not be accepted by users if it does not meet user expectations for quality: promptness, responsiveness, and cost effectiveness. Librarians need to be aware that TQM is not a tool for solving problems as they occur in the work processes. Nevertheless, TQM can prevent problems as service continues to improve by ensuring quality productivity and service executed in a consistent manner.

CONCLUSION

Challenged by commercial information services, information users, and technological advances, today's ILL and document delivery librarians must engage in TQM to forge a new sense of tomorrow's information services. Unlike past generations, ILL in the electronic age has become customer driven and technology driven service. Librarians must possess a whole new set of responsibilities in order to transform traditional ILL service. This process involves managing for total quality service and productivity, designing and planning for value-added service, adapting new information technology, marketing and promoting services, and developing information delivery systems. Most of all, in today's electronic age, librarians must be competitive in positioning and marketing ILL and document delivery services. As Eldred Smith and Peggy Johnson state, "interlibrary loan must be overhauled, expanded and moved front and center with research library facilities, priorities, and budgets. It must be staffed with some of the library's most effective, most service-minded personnel."[15]

As computer technology continues to improve and the economic outlook remains uncertain, the ultimate venture is not just how to deliver materials to users, but rather how to outsource in order to optimize service value. To do so, administrators and ILL librarians must articulate high-tech, high-quality ILL and delivery services, attain a breadth of service perspective, and, above all, envision new options for achieving TQM.

REFERENCES

1. Lloyd Dobyns and Clare Crawford-Mason, *Quality or Else*, (Boston: Houghton Mifflin, 1991), 2.

2. Barbra Buckner Higginbotham and Sally Bowdoin, *Access Versus Assets*, (Chicago: American Library Association, 1993), 17.

3. Dobyns and Crawford-Mason, 238.

4. John V. Lombardi, " With their Accounts in Order, Colleges Can Win Back Their Critics," *The Chronicle of Higher Education*, 17 Feb.1993, A40.

5. John Naisbitt, *Megatrends: Ten New Directions Transforming Our Lives*, (New York: Warner,1982), 24.

6. David P. Hamilton, "Publishing by—and for—the numbers," *Science*, 7 December 1990, 1331-1332.

7. Naisbitt, 38.

8. Amy Chang, " A Database Management System for Interlibrary Loan," *Information Technology and Libraries* 9,(1990):135-143.

9. Michael Hammer, and James Champy, *Reengineering the Corporation*: A Manifesto for Business Revolution, (New York: HarperCollins Publishers, 1993), 90.

10. Leonard Berry, A. Parasuraman, and Valarie A. Zeithame, " A Conceptual Model of Service Quality and Its Implications for Future Research," *Journal of Marketing*, 49, no.4, (1985): 41-50.

11. David A. Garvin, "Quality on the Line," *Harvard Business Review*, 61, no.5 (1983): 65-75.

12. Will Kaydos, *Measuring Managing and Maximizing Performance* (Cambridge: Productivity Press, 1991): 24.

13. Jessica Keyes, *Infotrends: The Competitive Use Of Information,* (New York:McGraw Hill, 1992), 24.

14. John A. Byne, "Paradigms for Postmodern Manager," *Business Week/Reinventing America,* Special Issue, (1992): 63.

15 Eldred Smith, and Peggy Johnson," How to Survive the Present while Preparing for the future: A Research Library Strategy," *College & Research Libraries* 54, (1993): 393.

AVISO: AN INNOVATIVE INTERLIBRARY LOAN
MANAGEMENT SYSTEM

Dave Binkley
System Librarian/Analyst
Simon Fraser University

OVERVIEW

The phenomenon is universal: acquisitions budgets have declined, electronic bibliographic access has been enlarged, and global information access has become reality to users. It all has made a great impact on every aspect of library services and operations. Most of all, interlibrary loan (ILL) has become a pivotal point in meeting the new demands for world information. Inevitably, the high volume of ILL transactions causes greater costs for libraries, and many libraries were not budgeting for such increase. The recent ILL analysis report indicates that staffing is a major contributor to increased costs.[1] Needless to say, this situation makes the ILL a natural candidate for automation.

In today's information world, enormous amounts of research information can be located and transmitted electronically. However, internal ILL operations, such as managing files, retrieving records, compiling statistics, bookkeeping, generating copyright reports, etc., slow the turnaround time of delivering materials. As personal computers become more powerful and cheaper, it is no longer a question of how these tasks can be automated, but rather of how to develop a local ILL management system that can interface with online systems and databases. This variety of tasks also means that an automated system should not be limited to performing one specific task, such as managing files or retrieving records; it should interact with a national bibliographic utility and other software packages for generating statistics and reports.

Four principles of ILL automation should be set forth:

1. Processing borrowing and lending transactions on the system, including statistics and bookkeeping work.

2. Importing data from another system, to eliminate re-keying of data.

3. Customizing to the various ways of operating ILL and enabling minimum change to work flow.

4. Maximizing the capability of the database for retrieving records, maintaining files, and generating reports.

A system that embodies these four principles must run on a widely available and

64

inexpensive platform, must coexist with a variety of local library systems, and must interface with the diversity of function and external data sources. This points to the AVISO software program for ILL management, a computerized system that has simplified and streamlined the complexity of ILL operations.

AVISO: HISTORY AND STRUCTURE

The AVISO ILL program was first developed by this author in 1986 at the University of Waterloo in Ontario, Canada, where the author supervised the Dana Porter Library ILL operation. AVISO began with a database routine running on an Osborne computer that tracks ILL billing based on reciprocal agreements at the University of Waterloo. Over the years, with input from over fifty libraries across Canada, the program has been enlarged and enhanced, for example, patron database was developed into the program, and the system is able to parse in from the OCLC and UTLAS databases.

In 1993, ISM Library Information Systems of Toronto (formerly UTLAS International) Canada acquired the AVISO system, and since then, ISM has revised the program for the release of version 4 in the fall of 1994. It has approximately ninety customers in addition to Ontario. The sample screens reproduced in this article are from the pre-ISM version (3.51).

AVISO comprises some 16,000 lines of code, distributed as a stand-alone, compiled program. A DOS batch file is used for program launching, and PROCOMM or Kermit scripts for communications. Assembler and C routines have been added for record capture and batch uploading of Internet mail. FoxPro, Microsoft's entry into the x-base language arena, provides a flexible, high-level, database-oriented programming environment, well suited to the development of a wide-ranging, complex system. AVISO also takes advantage of FoxPro's LAN support for multi-user installations. It is expected that AVISO will eventually be able to implement the multi-platform support that Microsoft has announced for FoxPro to run on UNIX.

INTERLIBRARY LOAN PROCESS

AVISO is distinguished by its attempt to automate the entire ILL process and to provide a single point of access to the variety of external systems with which the ILL operator must contend. The ILL process functions are outlined in Fig. 7.1: verification of the patron and the requested item; messaging to the lending library to acquire the item; circulation of the item to the patron and, in the case of returnables, back to the supplying library; and accounting, which includes the generation of financial and statistical reports.

These functions use a variety of computer systems, both within and outside the library, as illustrated in Fig. 7.2a and 7.2b. Bibliographic utilities, specifically provide bibliographic information, locations, and a means of transmitting the request to holding libraries.

Commercial document delivery services, such as the UnCover service, are becoming a widely used source of obtaining research material. The local OPAC is used

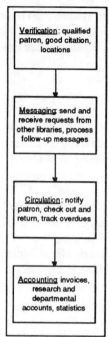

Figure 7.1: The ILL Process

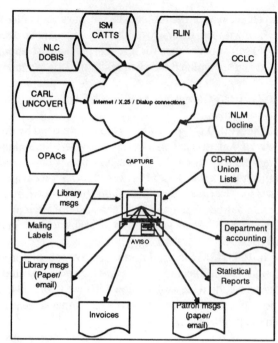

Figure 7.2a: The World of ILL

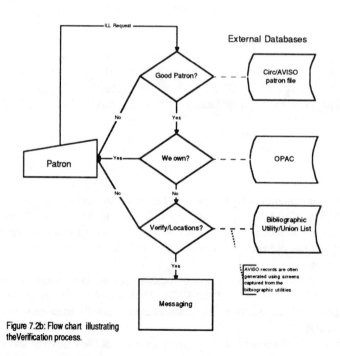

Figure 7.2b: Flow chart illustrating
the Verification process.

66

to determine whether or not items are held, and other libraries' OPACs can be used for locations. The circulation system contains patron information, and electronic mail of various types is used to communicate with other libraries and with patrons.

While this essay is written largely from the perspective of the borrowing library, it should be kept in mind that there are equivalent functions from the lending library's viewpoint: verification that the requesting library is qualified to borrow and that the item is held and available for lending; messaging to receive requests and to alert borrowers to unfilled requests; circulation of items to requesting libraries; and financial and statistical accounting, primarily invoicing.

AVISO FILES

AVISO is built around a cluster of databases (Fig. 7.3), which replace the myriad paper files that most ILL offices maintain: transactions, directories of libraries, patrons, statistics, archives of completed requests, and local library addresses and policy information. This process can be handled by either entering/parsing in from various text files, or creating a variety of formatted output from the databases.

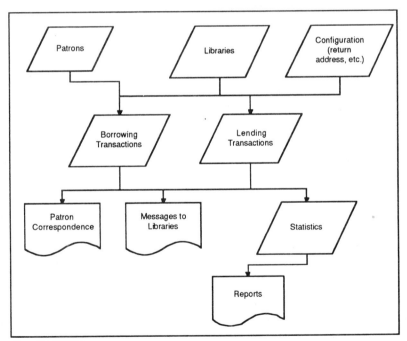

Figure 7.3: AVISO Files

The central file is the transaction file (Fig. 7.4). It divides into borrowing (items acquired from other libraries), and lending (items supplied to other libraries). Each transaction record contains

- the bibliographic description of the requested item;
- the service requested (loan, copy, microform, etc.);
- the name of the patron who requested it (Full patron information is stored in the patron database.);
- the codes of other libraries involved in the transaction (Again, full information is stored in the library database.);
- the history of the transaction (An entry to the history field is added every time an action is performed so that we may easily review everything that has been done to an order.);
- copyright compliance and need-before date information;
- a code defining the member of the ILL staff to whom this transaction "belongs"; and
- notes

```
-01/01/94: Req from: BVAU-----------------Rev: 22/01/94-----Ord: S93120422-----
Patron: Binkley          , Dave          Date (dd/mm/yy): 21/11/93
Req [L=Ln X=Phot F=FAX A=Ariel B=Bind M=MicLn C=MicCop V=Vid U=Aud R=Mach R]: A
Item type [1=Book 2=Journal 3=Thesis 4=Report 5=Conference 6=Other]: 2
-Need before (dd/mm/yy):  / / -------Copyright: -------------Operator: 0---
Journal Title: Filmkritik.

Vol/No: v. 9 n. 4
Date: April, 1965              Pg: 168-209
Article Author: Gregor, Ulrich.

Article Title: Der blaue Engel.

Sponsoring body:

Verification: OCLC

Note [TAB:
  quits]
Cost: $  0.00Currcy: CAD   Acct #:          No of exps:  33
LCCN:        ISN:          Dobis No:
  OCLC No: IL 57162              RSN:
Forward----Back--Save---Quit request-----Note----Edit--------Delete------History-
Message---In--Out--$$-Check out--Renew--Cancel--Patron notice----Rev date-Rush--
```

Figure 7.4: Transaction Record Screen

The ILL transaction file interacts with patron and library databases. This interaction enables statistics to be generated by different categories. Additionally, the patron database includes the following information:

- department
- account number (This is used to assign charges for a patron to a departmental account or research grant and may be over-ridden for any particular order)
- a "flag", which pops up a note whenever the operator places an order on behalf of the patron

- running totals of completed orders and cost. (This allows a flag to be set to alert the operator when a patron has exceeded a particular number of orders or amount of money.)

These messages are necessary for the generation of patron notifications and e-mail messages illustrated in Fig. 7.5.

The library database (Fig. 7.6) includes

- two statistical categories,
- an account number for borrowing and lending to track deposit accounts,
- a "Branch" category to link a library to another library for billing and statistical purposes,
- a "flag" to record holiday closings and other temporary information.

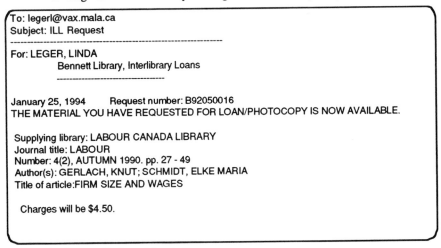

```
To: legerl@vax.mala.ca
Subject: ILL Request
-----------------------------------------------------------------
For: LEGER, LINDA
        Bennett Library, Interlibrary Loans
        -----------------------------


January 25, 1994        Request number: B92050016
THE MATERIAL YOU HAVE REQUESTED FOR LOAN/PHOTOCOPY IS NOW AVAILABLE.

Supplying library: LABOUR CANADA LIBRARY
Journal title: LABOUR
Number: 4(2), AUTUMN 1990. pp. 27 - 49
Author(s): GERLACH, KNUT; SCHMIDT, ELKE MARIA
Title of article:FIRM SIZE AND WAGES

  Charges will be $4.50.
```

Figure 7.5: Email patron notification ready for uploading

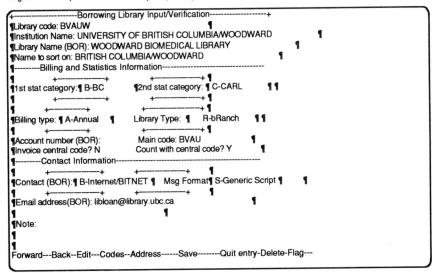

```
+--------------------Borrowing Library Input/Verification--------------------+
¶Library code: BVAUW                        ¶
¶Institution Name: UNIVERSITY OF BRITISH COLUMBIA/WOODWARD        ¶
¶Library Name (BOR): WOODWARD BIOMEDICAL LIBRARY              ¶
¶Name to sort on: BRITISH COLUMBIA/WOODWARD              ¶
¶--------Billing and Statistics Information-----------------------------
¶     +------------+ ¶    +------------+ ¶
¶1st stat category:¶ B-BC    ¶2nd stat category: ¶ C-CARL    ¶¶
¶     +------------+ ¶    +------------+ ¶
¶     +---------+        +------------+ ¶
¶Billing type: ¶ A-Annual   ¶   Library Type: ¶   R-bRanch   ¶¶
¶     +---------+        +------------+ ¶
¶Account number (BOR):      Main code: BVAU        ¶
¶Invoice central code? N    Count with central code? Y        ¶
¶--------Contact Information-----------------------------------
¶     +------------+        +---------+ ¶
¶Contact (BOR):¶ B-Internet/BITNET ¶  Msg Format¶ S-Generic Script ¶    ¶
¶     +------------+        +---------+ ¶
¶Email address(BOR): libloan@library.ubc.ca        ¶
¶Note:                        ¶
¶
¶
Forward---Back--Edit---Codes--Address------Save--------Quit entry-Delete-Flag---
```

Figure 7.6: Library Record Screen

Other data files include an optional file of journals and their locations, which may be pulled into a transaction; files of local configuration information; archive files of completed transactions; a file to map various library codes to one another; and cumulative statistical files.

VERIFICATION

Under verification are grouped the functions that generally precede the placing of a request with another library (Fig. 7.7):

- determining that the patron is qualified to access the ILL service. Patrons must be registered and in good standing and must not have exceeded cost limitations. Ideally, there would be a link to the library's circulation system for patron records, as the AVISO patron database in large part duplicates the patron information on file there. Pending a patron extension to Z39.50 is not possible.
- deciding that the requested item exists as cited
- finding locations for the item

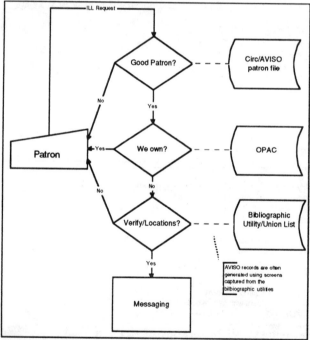

Figure 7.7: Verification process

Often the main source for verifying a request and determining which libraries hold the item is a bibliographic utility, such as OCLC, and ISM's REFCATS, or a CD-ROM union list, such AutoGraphic's Impact, or ROMULUS, distributed by the Canada Institute for Scientific and Technical Information. Ideally, each would support Z39.50, so the operator would not have to deal with a variety of interfaces.

Until Z39.50 becomes widely available, AVISO uses a specially written TSR utility to capture screens from these and other sources and to generate AVISO records without the operator's having to re-key the information. This TSR, called ACAP, can be popped up by the operator using a hot key while in any program that can be run on the computer. Thus, ACAP runs over a TELNET session to an OPAC, a CD-ROM session, an asynchronous session to a bibliographic utility. It is also able to prompt for patron and article information and to capture the screen to parse into the appropriate AVISO database. Currently, there are parsers for OCLC, ISM, ROMULUS, and IMPACT.

In some cases AVISO generates e-mail messages directly from the captured screens. In others, the request is transmitted using the bibliographic utility, and the captured screen is used only to create an AVISO record.

MESSAGING

Messaging includes all contacts between libraries, from the original request through cancellation and unfilled messages to renewal requests and overdue notices (Fig. 7. 8). In Canada, where AVISO was developed, electronic mail is the usual means of contact between libraries, unlike in the U.S., where the use of bibliographic utilities such as OCLC and RLIN for ILL requesting is much more prevalent. The National Library of Canada and Canada Institute of Scientific and Technical Information provided standard message formats, which made possible the automated parsing and generation of messages. From its inception, AVISO was required to generate and read the various standard message formats.

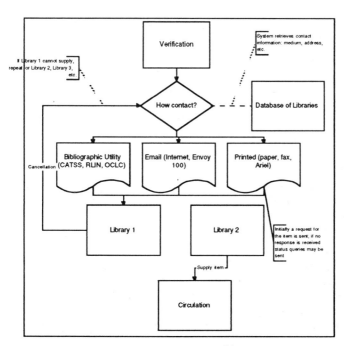

Figure 7.8: Messaging

In contacting another library, the first step is to determine the type of telecommunications to use and to verify as acceptable the type of message formats they expect. This information is stored in the library database. In the case of libraries to be contacted via mail or fax, a simulated ALA ILL form is generated (Fig. 7.9).

```
            +-----------------------------------+
       To: | WINDSOR PUBLIC LIBRARY             |
           | INTERLIBRARY LOANS DEPT, LIBRARY   |
           | 850 OUELLETTE AVE                  |
           | WINDSOR, ONTARIO                   |
           | CANADA   N9A 4M9                   |
            +-----------------------------------+

-----------------------------------------------------------
                   INTERLIBRARY LOAN REQUEST
Date: January 1, 1994        Request No: S93120422
+-----------------------------------------------+ |MAXCOST:
|Call No          |Simon Fraser University      | ||LENDING LIB REPORT:
|                 |Bennett Library, Interlibrary | ||Date Shipped:
|                 |                             | ||_____
|                 |Burnaby, British Columbia    | ||Special Instructions:
|                 |V5A 1S6                      | ||_____
|                 |Canada                       | ||_____
+-----------------------------------------------+ |
Request For: ARIEL transmission                  |
Patron: BINKLEY, DAVE                            | |RENEWALS:
                                                 | |_____
Journal: Filmkritik.                             | |_____
                                                 | |_____
Art Author: Gregor, Ulrich.                      | |Date Due:
                                                 | |_____
Art Title: Der blaue Engel.                      | |Not sent because:
                                                 | |_____
Vol/Num: v. 9 n. 4                               | |_____
Date: April, 1965                                | |_____
Pages: 168-209                                   | |_____
OCLC: IL 57162                                   | |_____
Verification: OCLC                               | |_____
```

Figure 7.9: Printed request as ALA form for mailing or faxing

The National Library of Canada led the development of what has become ISO 10161, the international ILL Protocol.[2] The Protocol uses a well-defined set of e-mail messages, along with a complex state table maintained by all parties to automate the exchange between libraries. By exchanging messages at each step of the process, the various parties to the transaction are kept abreast of the current state of the transaction. Matters internal to libraries, such as dealings with patrons, internal accounting, and connections with local systems, are not addressed in the Protocol. The Protocol does not include invoicing and statistics keeping. AVISO, in the ISM version, fully implements the ISO Protocol for transactions with other libraries, though it supports other messaging formats as well.

Once AVISO has determined from the library database how to contact another library, the message is output in the form of a text file, in the appropriate format. If printed output is required (that is, if the library must be contacted by mail), the format is a simulated ALA ILL form, and the file containing the request or other message is simply printed. For e-mail, a file of outgoing messages is prepared in a format that may be batch uploaded (one for Internet and one for Envoy). The same procedure—locating the library, determining the message medium and format, extracting the address information, and preparing the message—applies to the various follow-up messages. (see, for example, Fig.7.10).

A timer is used to launch a messaging session overnight. During this session

```
+----------------Choose Appropriate Answer Message-----------+
¶-Unfilled----Try later-----Conditional--Locations-Will supply  ¶
¶-Item Resrvd-Estimate---Shipped--Forward--Renew---Overdue---Quit¶
+---------------------------------------------------------------+
```

Figure 7.10: Lending Answer Message Menu Screen

upload, all messages that have been prepared <u>are uploaded</u>, and any incoming messages are read into a file for processing. AVISO comes with a utility called TCPMAIL, which uses the smtp mail protocol to batch upload Internet messages, and PROCOMM or Kermit scripts used for other e-mail systems.

CIRCULATION

Once the item has been shipped, another process takes over (Fig. 7.11). Circulation (from a borrowing library's perspective) conducts the following tasks:

- checking in items
- notifying patrons
- recording cost and statistical information
- checking out item to the patron
- collecting monies and tracking the various accounts to be charged
- tracking overdues and sending appropriate messages to patrons and
- returning the item.

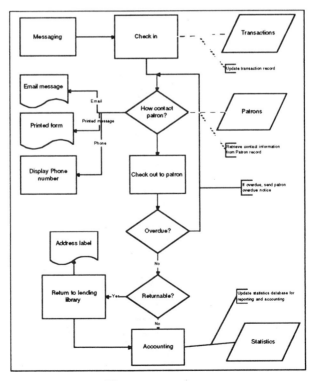

Figure 7.12: Circulation

73

AVISO generates patron notifications (see Fig. 7.5) either on paper or by e-mail message, assuming the patron has access to TCP/IP based mail. Overdues are calculated using due dates entered by the operator. The default messages for AVISO, such as the overdue notificati on to patrons or other libraries, the renewal request, or the patron notification slip, are stored in a database. Individual libraries can enter messages of their choice, which eliminates the need for all libraries to use the same wording.

Most of these activities are initiated at the check-in activity, that is, when the requested item arrives in the borrowing library.

ACCOUNTING

The statistical reports and accounting functions are derived from a separate statistics database. Every transaction (checking an item in, supplying an item, corresponding with a patron, filling a request, etc.) is recorded in the statistical database. A set of "canned" reports comes with AVISO, but since statistics files are geared toward events rather than transaction records, statistical reports may be generated on any action, combination of actions, library, or patron type (Fig. 7.12)— for example, all photocopies for undergraduates checked in from libraries of statistical category X between two dates. Statistics databases may be exported into various spreadsheets and other formats, or FoxPro's SQL report generator can produce custom reports.

Figure 7.12: A sample report

Bennell Library, Interlibrary Loans
01/07/93 - 31/07/93
MATERIALS BORROWED FROM THE UNDERMENTIONED LIBRARIES: 1st STATS CATEGORY

Counts orders checked in from these libraries.

BC Libraries	LOANS	COPY	FAX	MICRO	OTHER	ARIEL	TOTAL
B.C. RESEARCH LIBRARY	0	2	0	0	0	0	2
B.C. TELEPHONE COMPANY	0	1	0	0	0	0	1
BRITISH COLUMBIA ARCHIVES AND RECO	1	1	0	0	0	0	2
UNIVERSITY OF BRITISH COLUMBIA/MAI	115	327	0	1	0	0	443
CAPILANO COLLEGE	0	4	0	0	0	0	4
UNIVERSITY COLLEGE OF THE CARIBOO	3	10	1	0	0	0	14
COLLEGE OF NEW CALEDONIA	0	1	0	0	0	0	1
DOUGLAS COLLEGE	0	1	0	0	0	0	1
FISHERIES & OCEANS CANADA,	0	1	0	1	0	0	2
JUSTICE INSTITUTE OF BRITISH COLUM	0	6	1	0	0	0	7
KWANTLAN COLLEGE	1	0	0	0	0	0	1
MALASPINA COLLEGE	0	4	0	0	0	0	4
COLLEGE OF PHYSICIANS AND SURGEONS	0	3	0	0	0	0	3
OPEN LEARNING AGENCY LIBRARY	0	1	0	0	0	0	1
UNIVERSITY OF VICTORIA LIBRARY	12	17	0	1	0	0	30
WEST VANCOUVER MEMORIAL LIBRARY	0	0	0	0	0	0	0
WORKER'S COMPENSATION BOARD OF B.C	1	1	0	0	0	0	2
Sub-totals BC Libraries	143	391	2	3	0	0	539

CARL Libraries	LOANS	COPY	FAX	MICRO	OTHER	ARIEL	TOTAL
Sub-totals CARL Libraries	0	0	0	0	0	0	0
Sub-totals	143	391	2	3	0	0	539

EXTRA SYSTEM							
BC Post Secondary NET	0	0	0	0	0	0	0
Ontario Libraries	30	63	0	5	0	0	98
Quebec Libraries	5	11	0	0	0	0	16
Prairie Libraries	14	35	0	0	0	0	49
United States Libraries	52	62	0	6	0	0	120
International Libraries	0	0	0	0	0	0	0
Maritime Libraries	7	11	0	0	0	0	18
Sub-totals	108	182	0	11	0	0	301
TOTALS	251	573	2	14	0	0	840

CONCLUSION

AVISO has gone some distance toward providing integrated, comprehensive ILL workstation software, in accordance with the four principles introduced at the beginning of this essay. AVISO's strengths derive from its origins not in a software vendor's specifications, nor in the limited ISO ILL Protocol, but in a working ILL office.

To fulfill the needs for U.S. Libraries, AVISO is being developed within the guidelines of the NAILDD ILL/DD Management System Description.

The following features are highlights of the initial release of AVISO for U.S. Libraries:

- copyright compliance tracking
- data capture from OCLC and RLIN
- enhanced statistical tracking and reporting
- friendly screens

However there remains much room for future development, both within the AVISO system and in ILL operations, including the following:

1. A mechanism for patron-initiated request, so that patrons can either capture records from various sources or enter requests in a blank form. Development is also taking place in this area.

2. Document delivery options may be expanded to include scanned images included with e-mail messages. ARIEL has provided a model for the use of TCP/IP as the basis for transmission of articles. This approach needs to be extended to include a way to send documents directly to patrons. An initial step would be to build a seamless connection to ARIEL.

3. A completely flexible report generator to permit the user to produce on counts needs demand. AVISO allows the export of the statistical databases in spreadsheet and other formats and also supports SQL queries through FoxPro. However, experience has shown that users are not interested in investing the time to create their own reports using these tools.

4. An interface to a complete accounting package, such as ACCPAC, for those offices that require a high level of accounting. Ideally, this interface would include a means of electronic invoicing, perhaps based on a protocol like the BISAC standards.

It is to be hoped that ISM, in partnership with various members of the library community, will work toward implementing these and other enhancements to the AVISO software. Toward this end, ISM is working with the current customer base of approximate ninety libraries (recently expanded to include over three hundred fifty public libraries in Ontario) to improve the design of the product.

To have an ILL system based on an implementation of the ISO ILL Protocol come into wide use would be of immense benefit for the library community, even for those who do not themselves acquire the system, since such a system would give the vendors of library systems, many of whom are working on ILL systems, a de facto standard and common ground on which to come together. We do not need to see the barriers that incompatible bibliographic utilities have laid in the way of resource sharing being replicated by local systems vendors in their ILL modules.

REFERENCES

1. ARL/RLG Interlibrary Loan Cost Study: A Joint Effort by the ARL and RLG, June 1993, p. 28-29.

2. Fay Turner gives a general description of the protocol in "The Interlibrary Loan Protocol: An OSI Solution to ILL Messaging," *Library Hi Tech* 4 (1990): 73-82.

SWEEPING SAND AT THE SEA:
THE CHALLENGE OF STAFFING A GROWING SERVICE

Kathryn J. Deiss
Program Officer for Training
Association of Research Libraries

INTRODUCTION

Access is nothing new to libraries—it is, in fact, their very raison d'etre. The differences in how access is perceived, utilized, explained, and managed are what libraries today are attempting to define and integrate with their overall visions and plans. This is not a simple area either to define or integrate because so much of our effort has been centered on the issue of access versus ownership, rather than on the way access operates side by side with ownership. How libraries perceive their access services as part of their overall service mission is central to an understanding of how this broadening area should be budgeted for services and staffing. This new frontier must effectively manage the greatest boon library users have known: virtually unlimited access. This "management" implies optimizing the human resources allotted to access service activities. The wild success of the many access options is an opportunity to push our abilities to innovate even further.

INTERLIBRARY LOAN, A POSITIVE DRIVING FORCE

Overheard at an American Library Association conference: "Interlibrary loan hasn't changed—it's just more of the same!" I would say, "Think again". Interlibrary loan (ILL), and resource sharing, has become one of the major service points in providing information and research needs. Though full-text documents are increasingly available via the Internet, CD-ROM products, and commercial vendors, a large quantity of research materials, such as books, materials in special collections, scores, working papers, patents, newspapers, dissertations, reports, and proceedings, still need to be acquired from other institutions.

As the environment has changed drastically, affording users extraordinary increases in points of access and less real possibility of finding everything under one roof or even within one institution, many ILL librarians are evaluating the traditional ILL operations. The impact of electronic databases have been felt by ILL departments across the U.S. and Canada. Added to the hundreds of serial cancellations and/or cuts in monographic materials budgets, these new tools create a dynamic departure not only from the way ILL was accessed by library users, but from the very way that ILL services are performed. This essay will explore the changes in information technology and how these changes have affected ILL work flow, identify the staffing changes necessary for producing quality work and services, and discuss work relationships within and between the ILL department and other departments. Finally, it will examine the training needs for staffing and the leadership for managing resources and document delivery system.

TECHNOLOGICAL CHANGES

Students and faculty have responded robustly to the new information access and document delivery opportunities. This response has been reflected in the increasing ILL volume, as Mary Jackson and Shirley Baker state in their white paper <u>Maximizing Access, Minimizing Cost</u>, Association of Research Libraries (ARL) statistics show that ILL borrowing activity has increased by 206 percent and lending activity has increased by 155 percent since 1981.[1] The plateau many had predicted has not occurred.

Meanwhile, advances in the two major request transmission systems, OCLC and RLIN, have added new capabilities and introduced entirely new interfaces, (e.g., OCLC's PRISM ILL). This change has made an impact on how staff are trained and how workflow is handled. The ability to support laser scanning devices has allowed staff to update on OCLC very rapidly, but in many institutions, it has also triggered the charging of outgoing materials on local systems within ILL rather than in Circulation. New software packages ranging from ILL database management to Internet communication software have added new twists to the ILL workflow. As ILL volume has increased dramatically during the past few years, tasks such as collecting data for statistics, copyright compliance tracking, document transmission, citation verification, and the provision of collection management information can no longer be managed manually. Many of these tasks are now handled by software packages such as SAVEIT, Texas Tech's ILL Database Management, AVISO, and Brigham Young's "Patron Request System." The trick, of course, is that a trained human needs to manage the new work flow and direct the automated systems.

Fax machines represent as much (or more) change than photocopy machines did in their early days. So ubiquitous have fax machines become that requests from all types of libraries worldwide pour off these machines in growing numbers creating a new statistical and work-flow management category.

Aside from fax machines, a number of new transmission methods are now available to ILL. Two of these are the Committee on Institutional Cooperation's (CIC) PC/Fax Project[2] and Research Libraries Group's (RLG) ARIEL[3] document transmission software. Both of these products use the Internet to send documents to remote sites. Systems such as these directly affect staff by introducing yet another unintegrated tool into the ILL landscape. Keeping straight which libraries receive documents via which mechanism becomes nearly a full-time job.

Other technological changes such as CD-ROM local area networks and bibliographic indexes (e.g., IAC's Expanded Academic Index) mounted on the online catalogs pose new kinds of challenges for ILL staff. When faced with reams of printed citations direct from the CD products, ILL staff are aware, even as they describe the desired actions, that the clash between the sophisticated retrieval systems and the primitive requesting systems does not make any sense. ILL staff are in a position of having to uphold procedures that are clearly in need of innovation in order to meet the fast-changing environment for information needs. Even if this kind of anachronistic situation does not arouse frustration in the user, staff feels the stress of working in an environment that is at once sophisticated and archaic.

Looking back, it was not so much that ILL slowed down the process, rather it was the lack of an integrated ILL system or workstation and the lack of common standards within the technology in past years that has created an extremely complex environment in which ILL seem to be attempting to force many square pegs into just a few round holes.

These changes have been discontinuous, that is, not incremental but vastly varying in both impact and kind. This discontinuity caused by the technological changes makes ILL long-range planning even more difficult. Goals and plans might be developed, but a new software or new releases of old software or, new hardware, or even a new technology altogether can be disruptive to the long-range plan.

Such changes have not always been met with equal changes in the structure of ILL departments—in how the department conceives of the work, how the work is executed, and how it is viewed and supported by the library in general. As in any other venture, it is not sensible to change the technologies used to accomplish the work without looking at the appropriateness of the previously existing practices and procedures. The challenge is to employ mold-breaking thinking when adding new technologies and to thereby manage the impact on the service and on the staff supporting the delivery of that service.

CHANGES IN WORK PATTERNS AND JOB RESPONSIBILITY

Changes in technology have, in turn, called for alteration in work patterns and job structure. ILL staff is now more likely to have multi-task job responsibilities. In some cases, there may be great ambiguity regarding roles and the definition of an individual's job in relation to others in the department. The organization of the work has half changed to fit new equipment and ways of thinking about the ILL transaction, "half changed" because ILL departments have not fully entered the "virtual" era. The pastiche of old-fashioned and new-fangled creates a dissonant environment in which it becomes more and more difficult to explain precisely why we do something in a particular way.

ILL staff members are simply overwhelmed by the technological changes and dramatic amounts of work increases. At the same time, new work processes have not been developed to keep the pace of technological changes and to satisfy users' demands for fast service.

Lending staff, for instance, are working with several systems simultaneously These systems are unique and unable to connect to each other, (e.g., OCLC PRISM, local consortia database, OPAC, and other electronic databases). Questioning the need and benefit of every addition of a new technology or system is part of responsible library management. These systems are added on like beads on a string, but are not integrated. The whole is not changed as a result of adding the latest transmission mechanism—it reflects that the staff have to manage a more intricate set of possibilities and active systems, which requires more minute-by-minute judgment and discrimination than ever before. Lending, in fact, is perceived as the simplest and most direct of activities in ILL. Now, with many libraries being requested to send materials rush, fax, or via some other mechanism such as ARIEL and with reciprocal agreements, lending needs staff and management skills for work coordination more than in the past. Much training time is taken up learning the intricacies of the various online catalogs and mastering searching OCLC and RLIN. Work coordination is a difficult skill to obtain; it is among the most critical skills for a successful and productive lending operation, particularly in a complex technological environment. libraries lend more than they borrow; staffs are swimming upstream every day. The tidal wave of requests that came in yesterday is being worked on, while another tidal wave has today hit the shores of the lending operation. Most lending operations in the U.S. are woefully under staffed for the new age. The fact of the matter is that an increasingly wide variety of requests are coming in a broader range of formats and agreements and via an increasingly varying number of systems. Managing such complexity, ILL managers' major responsibility is managing staff and assisting them to succeed and to be able to take pride in the quantity and quality of work that they accomplish.

NONTECHNOLOGICAL CHANGES

One of the greatest changes that has occurred in ILL has been the steep increase in the number of consortial arrangements. These include state, regional, national, and one-on-one agreements governing how libraries will interact with one another. The type of material for loans, the cost to supply, the turnaround time, and the mechanisms for work processes are just some of the essentials of most consortial agreements.

For both lending and borrowing, various agreements require individual attention. Hundreds of requests must be sorted to differing priorities and agreements, and work flow must be managed appropriately and accordingly. This kind of organizational skill was not required a few years ago.

Additionally, billing and invoicing procedures are complicated by these nontechnical changes. Some libraries bill in various formats: invoice with the item monthly, or quarterly, or require payment in either their own coupons or in postal coupons. Though some software packages have check and invoicing modules, they can only be used partially since there is no universality in how libraries charge each other. It could take the majority of one staff member's time to maintain bookkeeping, including pre-payment orders, payment orders, and follow-up on unpaid invoices sent out.

Borrowing now is facing major changes. That is, staff works with the acceptance of borrowing requests, staff no longer work with requests that are as clear-cut as they once were. These requests often require consultation with the user. The consultation skill requires knowledge of reference sources, interpersonal skills, imagination, and the ability to spot incongruency. The increasing rich bibliographic information in the RLIN and OCLC databases as retrospective conversion projects are completed means a high likelihood of variant editions, translations, and details relating to specific items. Often users approach the ILL service for clarification and verification of a citation. Training ILL staff for this kind of activity is more akin to reference work than it is to a production line of automated requests. It is the balance between the rapid production line and the more detailed research consultation to which ILL staff should aspire.

Staff members in both borrowing and lending have to work cooperatively to ease such work load. Thus, cross training becomes essential in ILL. The side effect of the cross training is that it can increase the interactions among staff; and it will encourage a sense of teamwork within the department.

CHANGES IN WORK RELATIONSHIPS

As work patterns are shifted in ILL, changes in work relationships within and outside of the department begin to occur. These also need to be attended to, managed, carefully developed and nurtured, and acted upon using creativity and innovation. Too often we read about the changes that happen "to us," and not the changes that we have effected consciously. The better we understand the change, the more likely we will be able to envision the outcome and be able to adapt to it. Though many of the ILL changes have come from external sources (e.g., electronic information access, user expectations for services), ILL librarians have learned new electronic access, and some even influence using our expertise in accessing research materials through other institutions. However, creativity and innovation imply being expert enough in an area to identify either nonconforming data or coincidences in patterns. Staff should raise questions of not only how to do the job right, but also why they are doing it. They should face problems and then respect the process of testing ideas. This may involve risk-taking by the library administrators. Nevertheless, the process will assist in developing a strong sense of team membership that encourages innovation and creativity for problem solving. By developing strong group skills, new paths will be found through the dunes that drift above our heads. Team development can be time-consuming; often it is caused by the lack of encouragement of creativity that prevents ILL from actually moving in an effective direction.

Interdepartmental relations is another area that has impacted on work relationships. Ever since library implemented automated systems, levels of collaboration between ILL departments, such as reference, government publications, and branch libraries and other departments have increased, lines of responsibility have blurred and awareness of resources outside of the ILL department has expanded. This collaboration allows staff members to be trained in different departments such as preservation, reference, and ILL in order to gain broad skills.

In addition, ILL staff collaborates with the automation department in their libraries, as well as with staff at OCLC and RLIN, involving system troubleshoot and developing new ILL systems. In many cases, because of the hands-on experience in dealing with various electronic systems, ILL staff has more knowledge than the automation staff does.

The reference and library automation skills gained by the ILL staff have forced the collaboration effort between ILL and other departments and will eventually increase the efficiency in ILL.

STAFF TRAINING IN A CHANGING ENVIRONMENT

As we experience wave after wave of technological, nontechnological, work pattern, and work relationship changes, to prioritize one over another is difficult. Occurrences of these changes are actually mold-breaking ones. One of the areas that is ripe at this time is training. Are there new ways to learn tasks, new and better ways to relieve or redirect stress, to learn to work together as a team? Will these learning experiences have a positive effect on the end result, providing what users need? The answer to these questions may well be "yes." However, it requires the creation of more effective training programs that encompass more than narrow task accomplishment and that offer much more learning opportunities for acquiring new skills and adapting to changes. Each staff member must have an overall view in which libraries are sharing resources now and in the foreseeable future. This vision used to be considered the realm of the librarian and/or the administrator, now it is required by staff at all levels in ILL. Policy development, for instance, is an area in which staff should be involved rather than just asked to implement policies without context. At Northwestern University, the paraprofessional staff members were involved in the writing of a borrowing policy. The staff had direct influence on the policy based on their experiences and practices, and thus were very practiced. Besides, because of this intimate involvement in its creation, the staff have been better at applying the policy. Team skill development requires strong and well -thought out training programs and leadership skills. Organizational development instruments such as the Thomas-Kilmann Conflict Mode instrument, the "What Makes Your Team Tick?" instrument and the Myers-Briggs Type Indicator instrument, to name just a few, can be used to great benefit within the ILL department.[4]

The new way of forming team relationships within the department will address change by releasing staff to generate ideas for problem-solving. This may threaten the managers within a traditional authority structure; however, in a networked electronic environment, the conventional command-and-control management is much superannuated and should not be a comfort to us.

CHANGES IN STAFFING LEVELS

As libraries continue to face economic change, ILL managers and administrators must seek new ways to operate ILL cost-effectively. Thus, care needs to be taken in relation to staffing costs. Libraries should not look at ILL staffing costs divorced from the staffing costs of other service areas or from the costs of the library's overall priorities. An obvious case in point here might be the use to which individual libraries put the results of the ARL/RLG ILL Cost Study[5]. Though very interesting and thorough, it does not mean anything by itself; it needs to be placed in context to costs of other service areas, and it needs to answer the question of institutional context before it can be sensibly applied.

In general, what worked just fine a few years ago in ILL staffing can no longer work efficiently today. For instance, the stratified ILL department with clerical, library assistant, and paraprofessional and/or professional roles needs drastic revision. Whereas ten years ago a clerk/typist or filing clerk were reasonable and necessary positions, now the ILL department needs paraprofessionals with technical skills who are comfortable with more responsibility and who are flexible enough to accept the new multifaceted job description with enthusiasm. Today, there are single positions that encompass such varied responsibilities as computer troubleshooting and upkeep, financial management, database management, and service/productivity management. Positions such as these are necessary replacements for the clerical positions that existed in pre-automation days.

Staffing levels (i.e., the number of staff and responsibilities they hold), must change with the changing environment. Shirley Baker and Mary Jackson point out in their ARL white paper that "staffing levels have increased much more slowly than interlibrary loan traffic. The average of Interlibrary loan staffing rose less than 15% during the past five years, while traffic rose 45 percent or more."[6] What is the appropriate staffing level? What should be the ratio of student employees to full-time or part-time employees? How can staffing levels be made to fit an environment in which there is very little slow time anymore; summers and intersessions are almost as busy at many institutions' ILL departments as regular semester and quarter periods. Libraries most often base appropriate staffing levels on two unreliable tenets: first, if the department is "functioning" with the staff it has, everything is OK and second, if another library's staffing level is different and they seem to be "functioning", then that is what should exist at one's own institution. Many ILL staff have faced that they are doing more with less. There are no prescriptive staffing standards for university and research libraries, the powerful staffing standards documents such as the ACRL Staffing Standards for University Libraries can assist a library in analyzing its situation for adequate staffing.[7] Most of these standards documents call for the library to place its staffing needs in a context shaped by its vision, its overall plan of action, its priorities. This context is sadly lacking in envisioning such developments for ILL in order to meet the demands placed on staff. Determining appropriate levels of ILL staffing requires the same attention and support as other departments in the library from the administrators at all levels.

LEADERSHIP IN MANAGING INTERLIBRARY LOAN

The need for team development strategies, discussed above, implies a participatory management style. When most library managers/supervisors are asked what their management style is, they are unlikely to say "autocratic"; instead, they are much more likely to state that it is an inclusionary style, a participatory style. But are managers and staff prepared to use participatory management effectively? With the stresses of incoming and outgoing requests and materials at an all-time high, ILL staff—including the manager—are not likely to have the time to put into considered planning and discussion of issues. This means that rather than participatory management, these operations are running by the "seat of the pants" management style. This is not to say that the talent is not there, nor that many ILL librarians and their staff do not try to set up participatory climates. But, it is nearly impossible to accomplish this change given the current levels of demand coupled with existing outdated staffing level. The old mold needs to be broken. Staff need to be able to spend time on improving service by actively solving problems through teamwork and concept development.

This means that work teams need to be put in place with strong leadership, and new training programs need to be designed. It also calls for much more work with staff. Humans are not, as a rule, very comfortable with ambiguity and dramatic change; thus strong and supportive leadership of the ILL department is critical. Staff needs to be able to express concerns, but still be able to move forward and put in motion new and, perhaps, unreliable processes. Leadership is also increasingly available within the staff itself. This new possibility should be taken advantage of while keeping the larger institutional context in mind. Leadership development should be a continuous education through in-house training or training programs provided by ARL/OMS and other organizations.

CONCLUSION

Many libraries have considered and/or enacted centralization of ILL. This structure made a certain degree of sense, especially when statistics keeping was by and large a manual effort, when dedicated terminals were at a premium, and when branch libraries did not have the staff to train and to devote to a non-central activity. Now that terminals are cheaper, access has proliferated with campus networking, and the swiftness of delivery has become increasingly important, decentralization begins to look like a more rational way of managing a large volume of requests campus-wide. There is a great deal of room for innovation in ILL, and the ILL staff and other branch staff should be encouraged to discuss these issues as a potential moldbreaker. Another organizational structure option could be the merge of ILL and other departments in order to optimize staff levels within the library. Although this solution may not be ideal for ILL operations, and the restructuring may require large amounts of time for staff training, for the benefit of maximizing resources in the library, a number of libraries have either enacted or are considering it.

The question of how best to increase staff capability for high productivity has been a challenge to library administrators and calls for a rigorous look, especially at staffing as it relates to institutional public service priorities.

REFERENCES

1.   Shirley K. Baker, and Mary E. Jackson. Maximizing Access, Minimizing Cost: A First Step Toward the Information Access Future. Report to the ARL Committee on Access to Information Resources (Washington D.C. Association of Research Libraries, 1992), 3.

2.   The Committee on Institutional Cooperation (CIC) libraries comprise those libraries at the Big Ten universities and the University of Chicago and Pennsylvania State University. The CIC PC/Fax Project was developed by Ohio State University's Academic Computing and Networking Service in conjunction with the CIC libraries and with support from the central CIC office in Urbana, Illinois. It is a document transmission system using software, computers, and fax machines to transmit over the Internet.

3. ARIEL is software available from the Research Libraries Group in Mountainview, California. It uses scanners, laser printers, and a microcomputer with ethernet capabilities to scan, print, and transmit documents via the Internet. The quality of the transmission is extremely high compared to ordinary fax transmission.

4. The Thomas-Kilmann Conflict Mode instrument is widely used to help individuals realize the many different ways of responding to conflict and to stimulate discussion regarding particular behaviors within groups. It is published by Xicom, Woods Road, Tuxedo, NY 10987 tel. 800-759-4266. *What Makes your Team Tick?* is an instrument designed to show individual tendencies within team work phases and team roles. In addition, it is a strong instrument for use with an entire group. Designed by Frederick S. Mumma, it is published by Organization Design and Development, Inc. through *The HDR Quarterly*, 2020 Renaissance Boulevard, Suite 100, King of Prussia, PA 19406, tel. (215) 279-2002. The Myers-Briggs Type Indicator is a widely used instrument that assists individuals in seeing their own tendencies more clearly and in understanding where they get their energy from and how they make decisions. It is available only through certified consultants.

5. The ARI/RLG Interlibrary Loan Cost Study was an extensive effort to determine the per-loan and per-borrow costs of ILL transactions. Data gathered from each institution participating were put through a computer program that identified the transaction costs based on the "true" overhead of the ILL department. These Figures are not easy to compare cross-institutionally due the wide variation in practices, campus geographies, and staffing. They do, however, give each library a fairly accurate figure with which to work.

6. Baker and Jackson 7.

7. Association of College and Research Libraries (ACRL). "Standards for University Libraries: Evaluation of performance," *College and Research Libraries News*, 8 (Summer 1989), 679-91.

MANAGING INTERLIBRARY LOAN OPERATIONS:
A SUCCESSFUL EXPERIENCE IN AN ACADEMIC LIBRARY

Martha Steele
Head of Access Services
University of Houston

Keiko Horton
Coordinator of Interlibrary Loan Service
University of Houston

INTRODUCTION

Was it so very long ago that most interlibrary loan offices were relegated to a small, quiet work area of the library where requests were processed manually? Back then, only a handful of patrons knew about and used interlibrary loan services because local collections were the major source to fill research needs.

When computer communications were introduced into interlibrary loan operations, access to current holdings of libraries nationwide expanded, and a dramatic improvement in turnaround time occurred.[1] Ever since this revolution of sharing resources among libraries, interlibrary loan (ILL) departments have experienced a steady increase in the number of requests received, both from their own users and from users of borrowing libraries. Other pressures contributing to the increase in requests are rising materials costs, static or decreasing library budgets, and improving bibliographies. Certainly, current technological advances have opened up quick and easy access to many sources, and patron expectations for faster delivery service are rising.

Faced with an increased workload and little or no increase in funding, ILL departments are seeking ways to improve work design and thus increase productivity. (Productivity is defined as the ratio of output to input, or the ratio of effectiveness to efficiency.)[2] This essay introduces the successful experience at the University of Houston (UH) Libraries of restructuring work flow, rearranging physical facilities, and automating operations. Re-engineering ILL work flow involves management techniques such as subjective task analysis, Total Quality Management, and value analysis.

SUBJECTIVE TASK ANALYSIS

Before restructuring and redesigning the ILL process at the UH, a series of questions was developed.

1. What is the goal of interlibrary loan operations? Generally interlibrary loan departments share a common goal: provide prompt document delivery service.

2. What happens to each interlibrary loan request from the moment of receipt to the moment it is considered completed? What are the costs involved in performing each task? Can the task be performed in a less costly manner?
3. Why is a particular task being done? Is this task really necessary to accomplish the objectives of the department?
4. How efficiently is the task being performed? Can it be simplified, modified, or even eliminated? Can any bottlenecks be identified? How should work flow be modified to remove these bottlenecks? Can the task be broken down into smaller tasks? Can a task being performed manually be automated? Is there better equipment or software available? Would a rearrangement of equipment and furniture improve the work flow?
5. Where is the task performed? Would another location make the job easier? Is another department better equipped to do the work or now involved in similar processing?
6. Who does the work? What training is required to perform the task, and are those performing the task qualified? Do they require more training, or are they overqualified? Who does the training, and is the trainer qualified? How much training is optimal? Who is monitoring the work flow to verify that all steps are performed in a satisfactory way? How should managers evaluate staff who are performing the work?
7. What is the mechanism of processing requests? How often is the work performance monitored?

The objective of answering these questions was to eliminate any unnecessary or duplicated tasks and to simplify, combine, or improve existing tasks.[3]

Subjective task analysis offers some specific procedures to follow in order to elicit the information that managers need to answer the questions posed above. This type of analysis encourages employees to develop improvements for job designs, and may be especially appropriate for long-term employees who may feel threatened by the change implied in the process of examining the work flow. A key to success is objective and perceptive listening on the part of the manager and participation of all staff members. When the manager is not responsive to staff suggestions, he/she may ignore important management information, and thus discourage future contributions from staff.

The subjective task analysis involves:

1. Evaluation of each task in the unit. Staff are asked to list all tasks performed in the department. The manager selects the criteria by which tasks are to be evaluated, and staff members meet as a group to evaluate each task.
2. Development of alternatives. Staff are encouraged to propose suggestions for improvements. All alternatives are considered in order to develop creative solutions. If suggestions are discarded as impractical at this point, it may discourage other, more practical suggestions.
3. Evaluation of alternatives, assessment of skills needed and skills available to the unit, and selection of the best of the alternatives. At this stage, each

alternative is critiqued, and the best alternative selected. Skills and experience of members of the group are then assessed to determine the assignment of tasks. Tasks considered undesirable are examined for ways to make them more pleasant, and the group's evaluation is taken into consideration when formulating each individual job.

4. Flowcharting of new processes. Before implementation, the job designs should be flowcharted in order to ensure that all steps are included. Then, the design must be tested to make sure that the new models accomplish what is intended and improvement is achieved.[4] These are followed by testing of new processes, and implementation of the selected alternatives.

TOTAL QUALITY MANAGEMENT (TQM)

"TQM is a system of continuous improvement employing participative management and centered on the needs of customers."[5] TQM is the current management strategy that allows the development of efficient work flow within an organization. However, take into account that "TQM is about fundamental, cultural change which cannot be accomplished overnight, or in a year, though positive changes . . . should occur early in the process."[6]

In institutions that are to adopt TQM, the interlibrary loan department is an ideal target for first-year goals. Many works on TQM recommend "gathering the low-hanging fruit first," the metaphor for prioritizing customer demands that are easily identified and readily satisfied. Based on users' demands, two functions are served in ILL: obtaining materials not available at the local library and providing materials to other libraries upon request. Measures for service quality improvement, such as percentage of requests filled vs. unfilled requests and the turnaround time, can be easily conducted in ILL.

Once users' needs are determined, the TQM method calls for forming teams. In some cases, the team should include staff members from other departments, especially if other departments are responsible for a component of ILL service. Each team is given the task of improving the processes needed to deliver the service. Team members should be instructed in using TQM tools (e.g. cause and effect analysis, Pareto charts and fishbone diagrams for analyzing data, and flowcharts and Gnatt charts for problem solving, quality improvement, and planning improvements).

TQM also includes judging quality by using comparative assessment with similar organizations. This process is called benchmarking, and in interlibrary loan service the points of comparison are fillrates, delivery time, and costs of service. Fillrates are documented in a study published by the ARL Office of Management Services entitled Interlibrary Loan in Academic and Research Libraries: Workload and Staffing.[7] This report can be used as a tool to define the quality of ILL service. The ARL/ RLG Interlibrary Loan Cost Study can be utilized as a benchmark for cost management.[8] OCLC supplies data on turnaround time and fill rates for requests transmitted via OCLC. Frequently, local library consortia compare such data among themselves and sometimes develop standardized studies of costs, fill rates, or delivery time.

VALUE ANALYSIS

"Value Analysis is an organized approach to identifying what is needed from a function and redesigning that function so that it will reliably achieve its objectives with the lowest cost."[9] It involves the following steps in using this technique:

1. Define the objective for every task. When more than one objective is identified, the primary objective must be designated.
2. Rank the objectives for each function in the department according to its relationship to the basic objective. The cost of achieving the basic objective and each of the secondary objectives is calculated, based on time and other resources expended in performing the functions necessary to achieve the objectives.
3. Solicit alternative methods of meeting to meet objectives and performing tasks. The exact structure for developing these suggestions and evaluating them is not prescribed. The one requirement for this step is that managers must refrain from rejecting any alternatives without discussion and analysis. "The best alternative will be the one that balances objectives and user needs with the value of doing the function."[10]

These steps of analyses can be very time consuming. With the heavy workload in ILL, it is a challenge for managers and staff to find time to perform these analyses and to implement any improvements at the same time. As a starting point, staff can focus on problem areas where backlogs or bottlenecks have occurred. The important thing to remember is that a little time and effort spent on changes now should pay off in the future.

CASE STUDY

To illustrate, here is a description of an investigation at the UH Libraries that eliminated a particularly troublesome bottleneck in the processing of incoming ILL patron requests.

The UH Libraries requested 12,623 borrowing transactions in FY1990-/-1991, a 15 percent increase over the previous year. Until FY 1991-/-1992, two bibliographic searchers in the borrowing section of the ILL department performed the triple functions of searching the OCLC database for a matching record, assigning the lender string, and producing the ILL workform. As the workload increased and the searchers became bogged down with problem searches, tremendous backlogs accumulated. Several alternative solutions were tried in order to minimize backlog. A first alternative was to arrange the unprocessed requests in chronological sequence by date of receipt and then in alphabetical order by the patron's last name. If a patron inquired about the status of an unprocessed ILL request, his form was quickly located, and he was informed of the processing date. A sign was also posted on the front desk indicating the date of the requests on which staff were working. Requests for rush service were always honored and processed first.

Analysis of filled requests showed that half of the requests were found within the region served by the local courier service. Turnaround time from the point of first processing to the point of delivery to the UH library was only a few days, but many of these requests were not handled for a week, due to backlogs. A second alternative, was to process first those requests that we thought might be easily filled by libraries served by our courier service.

None of these solutions eliminated the backlog. Clearly, another solution had to be found. The coordinator of Interlibrary Loan Services contended that the initial search of the OCLC database would locate bibliographic records for a large percentage of requests received from patrons. A search assistant was assigned the task of quickly searching and locating records in the OCLC database, supplying the lender string, the patron field, and any special borrowing notes. He then forwarded these requests to a half-time clerk whose primary responsibility was to produce the requests on the OCLC ILL Subsystem. This practice has eliminated the backlog.

Requests that could not be quickly located on OCLC were passed on to a senior searcher who performed a higher level search of the OCLC database and also verified citations and locations in Ulrich's International Periodicals Directory, databases of the Library's Electronic Publications Center, online catalogs of library holdings available through the Internet, and other sources. Those that could be ordered using the OCLC ILL Subsystem were returned to the search assistant who filled out the workform and forwarded the request to the producer.

Requests not verified by the senior searcher were referred to the coordinator of ILL for the advanced-level searching or verification. Requests that could be ordered through OCLC after this next level of searching were put back in the main work flow described above. Requests that were to be prepared manually were passed on to a second half-time library clerk.

What were the results of this division of labor? Since FY1991-/-1992, the majority of incoming interlibrary loan requests submitted by the library's patrons receive initial processing within twenty-four working hours of receipt, in spite of the fact that requests now number over 16,000.

Due to the increase of efficiency, the unit cost at UH for a borrowing transaction was $12.78, compared with a mean cost of $18.62 and a median cost of $17.55 reported in the ARL/RLG Interlibrary Loan Cost Study.[11] This was in spite of a higher overall expenditure for OCLC and a higher aggregate cost for student employees. Savings came in the area of nonprofessional staff assigned to borrowing. The unit cost spent on non-professional staff was $3.63, versus a mean of $6.33 and a median of $5.23.

MANAGING WORK FLOW

As a result of the success of this technique of streamlining and standardizing initial processing of borrowing requests, a master plan was developed to apply this technique to the department. Standardized procedures obviously improve the speed with which work can be completed.

At UH, all work moves along an assembly line that provides a structure. Both lending and borrowing requests move from one step to the next. Those that are exceptional for any reason will be taken off the assembly line for special handling, but the goal is to get them back on the assembly line at the most appropriate point. For example, if a journal title consisting of a single word results in too many hits in the OCLC database, the title may be searched in Ulrich's International Periodicals Directory for an ISSN and if found, the request is returned to the assembly line.

The object of the assembly line is to minimize the amount of handling, since special handling is expensive and slows the completion of the individual request.[12] Special handling also makes status reports more difficult, complicates the logging of completion statistics, and increases the possibility of having requests "fall through the cracks."

As many tasks as possible should be accomplished using the assembly line approach. For example, if ILL staff orders documents from commercial document delivery suppliers, selecting those that offer access through OCLC eliminates the special handling that is necessary for vendors who do not offer this access.

Control mechanisms should be developed to allow the status of any request to be determined at any time. This control mechanism can range from something as sophisticated as an automated tracking system to something as simple as designated bins for requests needing special handling.

Quality checks are necessary to make certain that the assembly line is functioning at an optimal level. Every Friday, records in the pending file that have been outstanding for a month or longer are removed, status check is performed, and problems are resolved. If patrons still need the material, requests are initiated again. Other procedures include the sending of second "pickup" notices to remind patrons and the elimination of leaving phone messages with third parties.

Status requests from patrons are also treated as opportunities to check on the quality of our procedures. We may discover in tracking a request along the assembly line that all the procedures have not been followed correctly. Requests could have been removed from the assembly line and left on a staff member's desk, or borrowed items could have been received and accidentally returned to the lending library rather than going to the patron. A pattern of problems may suggest a flaw in the work flow. In such a case, the procedure would be modified to eliminate the likelihood of such glitches. In contemplating the implementation of an assembly line for ILL, staff members must first define tasks that are absolutely necessary to accomplish the department's goals. Then, the necessary tasks can be broken down into their component parts to standardize procedures. Staff must rank the importance of each task in the delivery of interlibrary loan service and determine the time frame required to perform tasks under normal circumstances. Also, procedures must be well designed to accommodate the exceptions that are inevitable.

Each task should be assigned to the staff member with the appropriate level of skill. Unless the volume of work in ILL is small, work flow is usually better organized when there is some degree of specialization. This is especially true in an environment of multiple bibliographic utilities.[13] At this point, examine the need for any additional training and develop necessary training programs.

Finally, the tasks of each staff member can be arranged in a checklist, with each person taking responsibility for checking this list daily to verify that each task has been performed. To maintain consistency, a master copy of the checklist should be used for sampling or spot checking. This can also assist in reviewing the operation for further improvement.

The structure that has been developed should be documented and, if possible, illustrated. In this process, one should adopt to the minimalist approach of "less is more" and the adage "a picture is worth a thousand words" in creating procedure manuals, which can also be used as training manuals.

The structure should also include contingency plans to be implemented in the event of planned or unplanned absences. Ad hoc reactions to predictable events such as absences are a threat to the efficient work flow. Use the master checklist to create contingency plans for each staff position by assigning duties of each employee to other staff members in the case of absences. Assume that there will be days when both employees will be absent, and therefore, multiple contingency plans should be put into effect. Then time will not be wasted on deciding who will do what.

In smaller libraries where interlibrary loan may be staffed by one or two employees, the administration must decide if immediate processing of interlibrary loan requests is a top priority. If so, staff from other departments must be part of the contingency plan. If there is no formal plan, then formal plans for dealing with backlogs must be developed. Will ILL employees be given overtime? Will they be relieved from other duties in order to catch up on ILL requests? If ILL has been delivering excellent, timely service, patrons have been conditioned to rely upon such service. Even in the case of a temporary backlog, patrons must be informed so they can modify their expectations.

How can staff perform these other duties when they are already overburdened with their own responsibilities? Staff may not be so resistant to increasing their workload during a temporary absence. It is amazing what can be accomplished on a temporary basis when the members of a department consider themselves part of a team committed to providing quality service. This team spirit should be cultivated during the process of developing work flow patterns when everyone is asked to contribute ideas.

Regular staff meetings are an effective way to learn if the work flow plan is functioning. They also provide an opportunity to foster the commitment to the department's service goals. But staff may be so intent upon keeping up with their daily responsibilities that they consider staff meetings disruptive. At the same time, they may continue to use routines that they recognize as flawed, simply because they feel too rushed to take time to develop more efficient methods. As an alternative to staff meetings, schedule individual meetings with each member of the staff on a rotation basis. In this setting, problems in the work flow can be brought up, discussed, and appropriate action taken to resolve them. This will reinforce the concept that each staff member is responsible for contributing to the efficiency of operations and, consequently, to the quality of service. Additionally, structures should be developed for responding to user's inquiries without causing interruptions in the work flow in ILL . To achieve that, ILL reception area should be considered; it should provide a focal point where patrons can receive assistance in filling out request forms and obtaining information on the status of requests. The reception area allows patrons to inquire directly to ILL instead of having their comments relayed by staff in other departments. It also allows ILL staff to share in the patrons' delight in receiving needed materials promptly, while at the same time bringing home the consequences of errors and delays in their work. The UH ILL reception area houses computers to access OCLC, online databases, Internet, the library online catalog, and the ILL manual, and other useful ILL reference tools.

At UH, to eliminate time-consuming telephone inquiries, a form letter was designed explaining the reason for the contact, requesting any additional bibliographic information, and specifying a deadline for receiving responses. The original request is filed under the deadline date, and a copy is sent to the patron. When the patron responds, the request is referred to the assembly line for further processing. This procedure accommodates late responses, but also allows requests to be closed out. Patrons are also notified if requests have not been filled or have been referred to another department in the library. This effort has greatly reduced the number of complaints about delays and inquires about the status requests.

Structuring staff for the specific task is critical to the success of an efficient work flow. Supervisors and/or office managers must be adept at customer service and employee management, and capable of using numerous print and electronic bibliographic sources. Senior bibliographic searchers must be individuals who enjoy challenges and problem-solving while adhering to a strict schedule. Those who perform preliminary searches must be skilled in using the database and undaunted by the repetitiveness of the searches. Producer of the ILL request work forms must be able to work quickly, accurately, and conscientiously.

In order for any work flow to function successfully, staff involved must clearly understand what their responsibilities are and how important it is for them to perform the tasks in a consistent, accurate, and timely manner. New staff should receive training regarding the work flow. Managers must emphasize the goal of ILL and the importance of meeting those goals. When the initial training has been completed, the supervisor should observe the new staff to be certain that the individual has understood the procedures and is performing them in a satisfactory manner. After that phase, a periodic spot check may be used to make sure that procedures are being followed and that the employee is performing at the rate established for each individual task.

Although staff are assigned to specialized duties, each member must develop a degree of familiarity and skill in performing other duties so that all work can be performed when absences occur. Cross training offers employees new challenges and the opportunity to "try out" for other positions.

INTERDEPARTMENTAL FUNCTIONS

In today's interconnected library environment, no department of the library works in isolation, and the ILL department interacts with other departments more than ever before. This change requires not only management skills, but finesse. Some changes for ILL work flow may affect operations in other departments and may not be initiated by the ILL manager alone. The ILL manager must be aware of any bottlenecks that prevent the efficient handling of ILL requests and document the situation in order to work with other department managers in making changes. For example, in many libraries, ILL requests are submitted at the reference desk. In this case, the up-to-date ILL policies and procedures should be supplied with any necessary explanations so that reference staff will understand the parameters of the service. The circulation or reserve department may be responsible for a number of ILL duties, ranging from retrieval of materials in fulfillment of lending requests to charging and discharging volumes.

In some cases, transferring duties to other departments leads to efficiencies. In other cases, taking on other functions may be the only way to speed the processing (e.g., an overwhelmed mail- room staff may not be able to rush ILL mail through, but packaging and labeling by the ILL staff may make it possible for them to improve their work flow).

PHYSICAL ARRANGEMENT ACCOMMODATING WORK FLOW

Although sharing resources has been a recurrent theme in library literature for years, many ILL work areas were designed before the electronic age for a much smaller staff and restricted services. ILL staff have found that working in a limited space for a growing operation and limited space can jeopardize the work flow and services.

But how do ILL departments manage when increased office space is not immediately available and they have to "make do" with the space that is currently assigned to their operations? At the UH Libraries, the borrowing and lending sections are located on opposite sides of the ILL work area with the OCLC and other terminals placed across the back end of the room. This arrangement has worked well to move requests smoothly and quickly along the assembly line. As ILL operations grow and the work space becomes even more crowded, the coordinator of ILL services constantly involves staff in the rearrangement of the work area, while maintaining the basic assembly line.

As mentioned earlier, a public reception area contributes to staff efficiency. The public services functions of ILL receive the attention they deserve, while the "back office" offers a quiet work area that allows staff to carry out tasks with a minimum of interruptions.

IMPACT OF COMPUTER TECHNOLOGIES

ILL managers must keep abreast of new developments in order to improve the quality of service. They must carefully handle the transition from the old to the new method by involving the staff, documenting the new procedures, and providing thorough training. Managers also need to be aware that incorporating new technologies may temporarily put a monkey wrench into ILL operations until they can be integrated smoothly into the work flow.

For example, ARIEL, an Internet-based image transmission system developed by the Research Libraries Group, has made an impact on ILL work flow. Once mate-

94

rial has been retrieved, a decision must be made about which documents are to be scanned for ARIEL transmission and which are to be handled by traditional methods. Incoming requests are reviewed by ILL staff, who color code requests to indicate how materials are to be sent, which requesting libraries are to be billed, and so on. In keeping with the goal of providing rapid document delivery, Ariel's benefits may outweigh the resulting increase in the work load.

Another technological impact on the work flow in ILL operations is the OCLC Microenhancer Software that prints bar codes on incoming ILL requests. Use of a bar code reader allows records to be updated more accurately and quickly. Printing incoming requests on two-ply carbonless computer paper and using one copy for updating and the other to accompany the document has eliminated the necessity to manually transcribe ILL numbers or to move materials from workstation. This step has also contributed to the overall efficiency of the operation.

As ILL operations grow in size, managers turn to automation to reduce the time and labor necessary to organize records, keep statistics, and generate various reports. A commercial database management system has been implemented at UH, which contains document delivery sources and information for locating materials not easily available through other libraries. Each record also describes the parameters for using a particular source, and gives details regarding costs, prepayment requirements, etc. The database has the keyword search capability which allows access to ILL staff in all levels. Some libraries have developed their own automated database management system for interlibrary loan, such as the AVISO, developed in Canada, ILL Database Management System at Texas Tech University Libraries, and SAVEIT.

A promising new project of the Association of Research Libraries targets technical enhancements for ILL, including ILL management software. This comprehensive software, under development by several library vendors, may result in significant improvements for ILL work flow. The report on this management software project, North American Interlibrary Loan/Document Delivery Project: ILL/DD Management System Description, is available on the Association of Research Libraries gopher.

CONCLUSION

The phrase "continuous improvement," a byword of Total Quality Management programs, is a good motto for interlibrary loan services, in which new developments are taking place regularly.

How do you fit continuous improvement into the day-to-day operations of the ILL department? Communication becomes a key in the on-going examination of processes. Regular staff meetings offer one opportunity to bring up work flow problems and improvement options. Introduction of any new technology is another opportunity to reconsider the work flow.

Henry Ford said that once a thing has been made the same way for six months, one should check to see if there is now a better way. If it was made the same way for two years, there has to be a better way.[14]

95

REFERENCES

1. Brian W. Williams, and Joan G. Hubbard, "Interlibrary Loan and Collection Management Application of an ILL Database Management System." *Journal of Interlibrary Loan & Information Supply* 1, no.3 (1991):85.

2. David Bain, *The Productivity Prescription: The Manager's Guide to Improved Productivity and Profit* (New York: McGraw-Hill, 1982), 3.

3. Robert E. Nolan, Richard T.Young, and Ben C. DiSylvester, *Improving Productivity Through Advanced Office Controls.* (New York: Anacom, 1980), 70-71.

4. Felix Frei, et al., *Work Design for the Competent Organization.* (Westport, Conn.: Quorum Books, 1993), 242-243.

5. Susan Jurow, and Susan B. Barnard, eds., *Integrating Total Quality Management in a Library Setting* (New York: Haworth Press, 1993), 2-3.

6. Jurow and Barnard 5.

7. Pat Weaver-Meyers, Shelly Clement, and Carolyn Mahin, *Interlibrary Loan in Academic and Research Libraries: Workload and Staffing* (Washington, D.C.: Office of Management Services, Association of Research Libraries, 1988).

8. Marilyn M Roche, *ARL/RLG Interlibrary Loan Cost Study*, (Washington, D.C. Association of Research Libraries, 1993).

9. Nolan, Young, and DiSylvester 71.

10. Nolan, Young, and DiSylvester 72.

11. Roche 1993.

12. Alicia M Morris, "Costs of Managing Exceptions to the Work Flow in Acquisitions Departments," in *Operational Costs in Acquisitions*, ed. James R. Coffee. (New York: Haworth Press, 1991), 21-31.

13. Ellen A. Parravano, "Use and Management of Multiple Bibliographic Utilities in an Interlibrary Loan Referral Operation," in *Research Access Through New Technology*, ed. Mary E. Jackson (New York: AMS Press, 1987), 22-46.

14. Nolan, Young, and DiSylvester 68.

THE LEADING/BLEEDING EDGE:
THE ROLE/TOLL OF LIBRARY STAFF
INVOLVED IN ELECTRONIC RESOURCE SHARING

Sheila Walters
Head of Interlibrary Loan and
Document Delivery Services
Arizona State University

INTRODUCTION

Anyone who works in libraries is aware that electronic access and retrieval is transforming resource sharing. Major academic research libraries traditionally are on the leading edge of the technological advances related to electronic document delivery. On one hand, library administrators and publicity will proudly proclaim state-of-the-art equipment and the glories of library services that are on the cutting edge of technology. Library staff, on the other hand, are more likely to refer to the new processes as bleeding edge technology because, in some cases, it is their jobs and professional reputations at risk. It is an era in librarianship that is as exciting and challenging to staff as it is frustrating. The focus of this essay is the role of, and the toll upon, those faced with the responsibility of bringing hi-tech document delivery to library units.

IMPACT OF INFORMATION TECHNOLOGY ON LIBRARY STAFF

Interlibrary loan and document delivery services (ILL/DDS) is the department that usually comes to mind whenever alternative access is involved. ILL/DDS is traditionally reputed (whether deservedly or not) to be slow and cumbersome, but enter the world of electronic resource sharing and staff are expected to perform miracles of instant access and delivery.

While the limelight seems to be currently focused on ILL/DDS, other library units also share a role in this new era of alternative access. Subject specialists are as often as not involved in deselection rather than selection of materials as serial cancellation projects increase across the nation. Reference librarians frequently face the challenge of identifying alternative resources when their library lacks the materials desired by patrons. Acquisitions staff faces the challenge of convincing auditors that monies designated for library resources are not misused when funds are siphoned off for access rather than acquisitions. Library administrators face the challenge of convincing accrediting review boards to take a qualitative rather than quantitative approach when ranking "virtual libraries." Instructional service and all public service staff are promoting instructing and motivating library users to access, and, in many cases, directly retrieve or order documents electronically. Most of all, the number of volumes owned, added, or cataloged is no longer relevant to the number of resources accessible; the percentage of document delivery requests filled and the speed of delivery in fulfilling those requests have become a effective way to measure the library's accessibility.

It is a seemingly endless challenge for staff to stay aware of a constantly grow-ing line of electronic resources, and regular re-training is required to learn the tech-niques required to use those resources acquired. The challenge is made more diffi-cult because many electronically accessible resources may not appear in traditional library catalogs --online or not. If ever a holistic approach was needed in managing libraries, electronic resource sharing calls for a unified team approach to meet the challenges and foray into the future. This essay will examine electronic access and articulate changing roles in ILL/DDS.

INFORMATION TECHNOLOGY

Staff with job descriptions related to information technology (IT) faces the chal-lenge of bringing access to electronic resources to library users, whether actually in the library or by remote access. Phase one is fairly standard--making one's own library holdings accessible to primary clientele. Decisions must be made as to whether or not remote access must be part of the system. Will it be on an internal LAN (local area network), or accessible to a wider network of libraries by dial-up access or other electronic means, such as Telnet over the Internet?

Resource sharing agreements with other libraries are virtually impossible unless there is READY ACCESS (as in seamless, invisible, user-friendly, and every other current buzz word) to the catalogs of all libraries involved. Not only is ready access to holdings invaluable, but for electronic resource sharing, today's OPAC must be linked to circulation records and provide patron-directed document delivery func-tions. Citations need to be captured and stored when found, then manipulated through actions that include checking holdings in one or more library catalogs. Enhance-ments should include retrieving electronically stored documents or requesting deliv-ery, interlibrary loan, or purchase of works, as needed. Payment mechanism must be included in the system, as well as a means of copyright monitoring when copying rather than purchasing is the chosen option.

Technical services staff also cope with the new resource sharing technology. The online public access catalog (OPAC) catches everything from the day the docu-ment is first ordered, through the claiming, receiving, cataloging or serial check-in, and binding processes, up to the moment it is on the shelf and ready for the patron to come in and use it in house or check it out. Whoa! Back up! This is the age of electronic resource sharing. While the OPAC reflects all of those processes, what about "virtual" library materials?

Cataloging details about available electronic texts is scattered. One "cataloged" inventory available over RLIN (Research Libraries Information Network) is The Rutgers Inventory of Machine-Readable Texts in the Humanities. It was cataloged according to standard Anglo-American Cataloging Rules for computer files, which are not well-suited to electronic texts; for example, they may lack a "title screen." The physical characteristics of a file may be less relevant to the library patron than information about software or hardware required to retrieve and/or manipulate the file.[1] Two excellent guides to electronic collections are BiblioData Fulltext Sources

Online for Periodicals, Newspapers, Newsletters and Newswires[2] and Directory of Electronic Journals, Newsletters and Academic Discussion Lists.[3]

CHALLENGES IN ELECTRONIC DATABASE ACCESS

The problem is compounded with electronic access to materials that a library may not own, but be leasing, such as full-text CD-ROM products like the ADONIS biomedical database or UMI's ProQuest databases. The dilemma is made more interesting when the library does not even lease the material, but still has almost instant access to remotely stored free resources on research networks. Articles on Dante's "Divine Comedy," for example, are accessible from Dartmouth College over the Internet, and information and articles on Greek and Latin classics archived electronically at Bryn Mawr College are freely accessible over the Internet.[4] Documents are easily delivered via FTP (file transfer protocol) to ILL or direct to the requester's home or office computer, if the user has Internet access. Many libraries mount databases that have document delivery order functions, such as UnCover, on the OPAC, providing added access to resources that may or may not be owned. Another option is access to full-text sources available online from other commercial services. Most libraries have established one or more accounts with vendors such as Dialog. Should a library add the titles in Dialog's Full-text Sources: Alpha List or Subject List[5] to the online catalog, with a note "For access, go to MARS (Machine Assisted Reference Services)"?

If so, the user should be warned that full-text is not always the complete article, much less the complete journal. The article will be text only, in most cases—no graphs, or illustrations, for example—and each full-text database producer makes decisions as to how complete the full-text product will be in comparison to the print product. Editorials, obituaries, reviews, articles for which the database producer does not have copyright clearance, advertisements, classified ads, articles that are too long (or too short) according to the database producer's criteria, and syndicated columns are a few examples of likely omissions from full-text online journals. How important is access to the complete edition for library users? Enough to make it impossible to cancel a print subscription to rely on the online resource?

What happens when libraries form a consortium for resource sharing purposes. Is John Q. Public expected to check each catalog in a separate database accessible on the OPAC under the nebulous heading "other library catalogs," or will a shared union catalog "simplify" resource sharing? Simplify it from the user's point of view; compound it from the cataloger's.

If a library does enter nonowned, but accessible, items in its OPAC, what happens when titles are withdrawn or altered in remote electronic archives? Jane D. Smith, with the Clearinghouse for Networked Information Discovery and Retrieval, describes many research network resources as "labors of love" that have the possibility of disappearing or being discontinued at the whim of the individuals responsible for the project.[6] Other popular Internet resources go commercial when the product becomes so widely used that the original producers can no longer afford the time involved in updating the document files or maintaining what may have grown into a huge archival database. The massive amounts of memory required to store large text files electronically (even more if graphic images are stored) caused many successful projects, which began as funded research, to move into the commercial sector in order to survive. Susan Hockey estimated that about 95 percent of existing electronic texts are in plain text (ASCII) format and are in the hands of individuals or research institutes; most were compiled for specific projects.[7] The remainder represent commercially available products, usually on CD-ROM or in full-text online databases.

Technological advances have improved scanning and storing techniques. Standards have been developed that surmount incompatible file formats. Costs for equipment have dropped enough to make the electronic publication of books much more feasible. We have seen only the tip of the iceberg with access to electronic resources. A major problem still to be resolved is whether resource sharing of electronically stored images will be allowed in the same way that print media are shared. Licensing agreements for software purchases are much more stringent than "fair use" guidelines for printed formats. On one hand, libraries that scan printed documents for electronic storage may be operating within fair use guidelines as long as only one copy of the work (printed or electronic version) is in use at any one time, but libraries that mount electronic files on LAN's for multiple access (electronic reserve or reference collections), for example, or libraries that make additional copies to send out on ILL must obtain permission to copy and pay required royalties. On the other hand, electronically stored non-copyrighted material is widening the realm of resource sharing possibilities, as formerly noncirculating rare books are often "preserved" in an electronic format that can be inexpensively duplicated or transmitted electronically. The possibilities for rapid fulfillment of international interlending requests, plus lower shipping costs, brings a gleam to the eyes of ILL.

While electronic databases are so popular, many are not particularly user-friendly. Reference staff may get so involved in lengthy sessions with database-related reference that they barely have time for patrons with "traditional" needs. It would be nice to say that such problems ease with time, that it is only the introductory period after a new service is brought up that brings chaos and frustration. Certainly, technological improvements in equipment are easing some problems. Juke-box CD carousels have eliminated much of the changing of disks. Z39.50 search interfaces make it easier to move from one database to another, regardless of one's subject expertise or lack thereof. But public service in an electronic environment is ever-changing. As soon as one concept is mastered, either the equipment changes, software is revised, or new functions are added. There is rarely time to catch one's breath between changes, much less actually gain confidence in one's ability to serve so many diverse needs.

Another effect of electronic document delivery is the impact on services to disabled library users. The passing of the American Disabilities Act had a significant effect on libraries, forcing a hard look at library service to the disabled. While most libraries have made architectural improvements that aided access to the library building (wheelchair ramps, elevators, etc.), ADA brought more attention to equal access to collections. Many of the services that improve access to disabled users focus on electronic access—voice synthesizers and large print online monitors for OPAC terminals. Electronic reserve collections also help make library materials available to patrons who can not easily come into the library (e.g., accepting telephone requests from disabled patrons and then delivering materials directly via mail, internal courier, or fax).

Many services that assist disabled library users have broader applications that may form the basis for library services to others as well. For example, a scanned document being downloaded to a computer disk is easier to manipulate and integrate into a research paper or publication—the very thought of which has publishers looking for means to control such actions. It is simply the electronic means of cut-and-paste techniques employed by writers and researchers for years.

ELECTRONIC ACCESS AND INTERLIBRARY LOAN

Another component of the information process is the actual retrieval of the documents desired by the end-user. The first electronic resources available in most libraries are usually bibliographical in nature—online catalogs, periodical indexes, and abstracts. Initially, due to the high costs associated with searching some commercial online databases, use was limited primarily to faculty or graduate students in the academic community and to the business community in public and special libraries. Online bibliographic searching on commercial databases was fairly rare in school and small public libraries. The advent of CD-ROM databases brought higher up-front costs (acquiring the hardware and buying or leasing the databases), but once installed , patrons had ready access, and the popularity of such services soared. Libraries that have introduced electronic resources have seen a change in user behavior. Patrons flock to these resources even when the database choices provide weak coverage for the research topic. Most databases manage a few hits on popular topics, even when the scope of the database is being stretched, but unless the patron questions the results, there is no opportunity for input from library staff. Yet, the end-user is probably judging the quality of library service based on the number of hits and the availability of the cited materials within the library.

Even when a database is appropriate for the topic, it is not always appropriate for the user. The English 101 student may marvel as reams of hits are printed off PsychLit on "public attitude towards people with AIDs," but what happens when the student tries to understand the clinical materials written for professionals in the field? What happens when the searcher discovers the library does not own all of the dissertations and clinical psychology journals that are the sources for the hits. Unless an appropriate reference interview is conducted, the student may be directed to ILL to acquire what the library lacks, instead of being assisted to locate suitable materials from among the thousands of appropriate materials owned. Alternative access complements other services; it is not a substitute for them.

A decade ago, many libraries did not offer interlibrary loan service to anyone but "serious" researchers. Restrictions on the number of requests that could be in process at any one time were also likely. Materials owned would not be borrowed from another library except under extremely extenuating circumstances; nor were popular, rare, or current materials likely to be requested. Publicly accessible electronic databases began to abound just about the same time that materials budgets in libraries began to shrink, and many of the restrictions on ILL began to be questioned. The path to the interlibrary loan office became well worn in most libraries. National and regional ILL codes are being revised to reflect the changing role of interlibrary loan. No longer is it strictly to supplement collection development, but now alternative access is recognized as an integral part of a library's resources. While the limitations on what can be requested by a borrowing library have loosened, the restrictions on what will be loaned have not changed as quickly. This means that some of these requests have potential for going unfilled or may have to be sent to several libraries before being filled.

There is still some misunderstanding about the costs of ILL and document delivery. The ARL/RLG Interlibrary Loan Cost Study reports that the average cost for a research library to borrow a document is $18.62 and to fill an ILL request averages $10.93.8 Paying nearly $30 per transaction should give pause for thought before using ILL as a substitute for the acquisition of inexpensive, frequently used items. If one considers the savings on the cost of the average book or subscription, plus processing costs to acquire, catalog, bind, shelve and circulate an item, plus the need for shelving or cabinets to house the materials in house, then ILL is still a bargain—even if it is not "free." When comparing ILL costs to commercial vendor offers, costs of purchasing hardware and software, subscribing the databases, staffing, and instructing patrons to access are often ignored.

RECIPROCAL AGREEMENT AMONG LIBRARIES

The concept of reciprocity is often misinterpreted to mean "free" rather than "balanced." Some libraries try to establish a "reciprocal agreement" with every library that will agree to one. The general logic behind this is that most ILL units are understaffed and rarely have bookkeeping staff to handle small invoices. With the cost to "cut a check" averaging $30, it is not cost effective to be issuing a lot of checks to cover the range $7 to $20 lending fees of non-reciprocal libraries. This is the logic that promotes the "reciprocal" concept. A few libraries modify the concept slightly and opt for a "reciprocal cost" arrangement; we will charge you what you charge us. Unfortunately, most libraries involved in reciprocal cost agreements usually forget to determine which lenders fee the agreement is based upon, the higher or the lower lending fee of the two parties. Other libraries exchange coupons, rather than payments, but net lenders tend to accumulate a lot of unused coupons. Rarely is reimbursement considered for net lenders except in state-wide or regional networks, where some libraries are designated net lenders. Even then, the amount of reimbursement usually averages under $5.00/filled request, nowhere near actual costs. Try to withdraw from such network, and a library's name becomes mud and the ILL/DDS unit is villainized as being more interested in robbing the poor than in fostering regional resource sharing.

The real meaning of "reciprocal" resource sharing agreements should NOT be based on the concept of cost-free interlending, but rather on a balanced sharing of collections—our library will supply your library with an item in return for your library supplying ours with something. While an item for item balance is unlikely, it should be within agreed upon limits. When a library consistently exceeds the limits, they should expect to be billed. At the least, they should not be surprised or offended if their "reciprocal partner" opts out of an imbalanced relationship.

Libraries that seek reciprocal agreements with all other libraries without considering the balance of trade fall into three groups: (1) net borrowers that will benefit by using other libraries collections more than they can ever hope to repay; (2) net lenders with regional networking commitments that override the imbalance in trade; or, (3) libraries that simply do not monitor the ILL process closely enough to be aware of the imbalance or realize what it may be costing their own library or their reciprocal partners.

Libraries in the first category should justify budget requests for adequate allocations either to develop collections that make the library more eligible for resource sharing agreements or allow them to pay for alternative access. Some net borrowers that consistently use the collections of another local library are said to "subscribe" to that library. The net borrower can either employ runners to go to the other library and copy materials or pick up book loans, or they fund an employee line in the other library's ILL/DDS unit to handle their requests. Couriers and electronic document delivery are often used to support an effective document delivery system for the net borrower without placing a burden on the lending library. Libraries in the second category may be locked into impractical agreements that can only be changed at the highest administrative levels, but certainly net lenders should be able to state a case for some level of reimbursement. The last category may not exist if net lenders knew that they would be reimbursed and net borrowers knew they would have to pay when an imbalance exists. Libraries would pay more attention when selecting reciprocal partners and would distribute the volume of requests more evenly.

Reciprocal agreements should form the basis of most resource sharing agreements related to an access versus acquisitions collection development policy. However, the partners in such agreements have to be as carefully selected as the book jobbers and subscription agents used in a traditional acquisition process. The scope of the collections, the methods of delivery, speed of delivery, and the fulfillment rate are far more important than the concept of "free ILL." Regional commitments may play a less important role in future reciprocal agreements than they have in the past. This is definitely true for the sharing of journal collections, where electronic scanning of documents and transmission over the Internet or via fax makes the distance between reciprocal libraries a non-issue. The same will become true of monographic sharing as more books are stored in electronic formats.

Reciprocal partnerships based on priority service to members have to be founded on a willingness to commit to state-of-the-art equipment and to staffing arrangements that allow for rapid processing of requests at both the borrowing and lending side of the process. Scanning documents and transmitting electronically is tedious and labor intensive, and requires competency in aligning documents correctly so that they are scanned right the first time. Few libraries can afford to be net lenders without being reimbursed, or without benefiting equally from rapid, reliable service from their suppliers. As collections develop or programs change, reciprocal agreements should be reviewed to be sure that the agreements in effect are still serving the needs of the partners involved. If not, it is time to cancel old agreements and seek new partners that are better suited to current needs.

COMMERCIAL DOCUMENT SERVICES

The expanding commercial document supply market may provide an alternative option to reciprocal agreements—particularly for current journal articles indexed or abstracted in standard bibliographic resources. In many cases, the titles covered are owned by a large number of libraries, but these are often titles in high demand in libraries and often off the shelf. It may be less expensive in the long run (particularly for net lenders) to drop out of imbalanced resource sharing agreements and utilize commercial suppliers, especially if they are experiencing a high level of unfilled requests from reciprocal partners.

Commercial document suppliers have been around over twenty years, but most have not been used heavily, except by special libraries. Past studies comparing interlibrary loan and commercial suppliers have frequently shown that the ILL process is as effective (and sometimes better) than commercial document delivery. However, the newcomers among the commercial suppliers have definitely shaken up the commercial document supply industry. There is much more competition for business, and quality of service is improving while costs are coming down for rapid delivery. More companies offer electronic ordering capabilities, and fax or electronic transmission via research networks is more likely to be the standard delivery mode, rather than a rush, special handling, added-cost feature. There is less need to go through an information broker to reach commercial services though "one-stop" shopping is still in its infancy. Services like OCLC's ArticleFirst document delivery service and RLG's CitaDel document delivery service allow a choice of suppliers and modes of transmission for the items selected for delivery, but the majority of commercial document suppliers are still vendor or product-specific.

Most libraries will benefit from a combination of reciprocal agreements with a very select group of libraries committed to equal service and commercial suppliers for the easily acquired documents likely to be in heavy use and off the shelf in other libraries. However, combining traditional ILL with commercial document supply usually requires some procedural changes if it is to be cost-effective. Most studies that compare traditional interlibrary loan with commercial document supply focus on cost and turnaround. Many libraries are willing to pay reasonable delivery costs to improve turnaround, especially if the delivery costs fall within the average cost to process an ILL transaction. After the results of the ARL/RLG Interlibrary Loan Cost Study was published, there seemed to be a surge of interest in commercial document supply as a supplement to ILL. If other internal processing costs could be reduced (less search and verification, less follow-up on incomplete or illegible copies, no copyright record keeping, for example), then the actual cost of a commercially supplied document might be no more than the average cost of an ILL. Improved turnaround would be the icing on the cake. That assumes, of course, that the commercial services will have a high fulfillment rate and that most requests will only be processed once by the ILL/DDS unit, if not removed from the ILL/DDS unit completely.

Selecting commercial supplier(s) or products that suit the library and patrons' needs is no easy matter. While cost and advertised turnaround are often at the top of the list of criteria, scope of inventory, ease of accessing the supplier's inventory, ease of ordering documents, mode of shipment, cost and availability of rapid document delivery, billing procedures, copyright compliance, and management reports all figure into the selection of a commercial supplier. Evaluating the supplier's service is based on turnaround, rate of fulfillment, amount of follow-up required, quality of copies received, ease of processing orders (including search and verification, ordering, processing materials upon receipt, and invoicing).[9] There are too many variables to predict which commercial supplier(s) will work best for any one library. The supplier that one library swears by is just as likely to be one that another library swears at. Service varies based on the completeness of the order citation; the dates of publication, publisher, and subjects ordered; equipment in use at the library for searching, transmitting and receiving documents; geographic location and time zones of the library and the supplier; mode of delivery; and even interpersonal relations between library staff and the supplier's staff.

NEW ROLE IN ILL/DDS STAFFING

For ILL/DDS staff who routinely search and order the majority of ILL requests on one major system, such as the OCLC or RLIN ILL systems, the switch to commercial suppliers is almost as dramatic as the changing role of the online computer coordinator in reference services, whose duties expanded from online computer literature searching to include the selection, installation, and use of a diverse array of additional electronic reference resources. ILL/DDS staff are being introduced to an ever-widening spectrum of document retrieval and document ordering resources, many of which require learning new searching or computer skills. Just being aware of the broad array and the scope of each resource is a challenge in itself. Full-text retrieval or document ordering is possible over "traditional" online bibliographic database providers, such as Dialog, but in the past, such searching was often the domain of reference librarians. Paraprofessionals in ILL/DDS who may be quite at ease searching and ordering over the national ILL systems tend to feel ill at ease when "paying by the minute" searching and ordering over other online systems. Perhaps the only difference is that Dialog, etc. provide the cost at the end of each search session, while OCLC, RLIN, etc. invoice monthly, and staff do not correlate the total monthly fees with actual transactions.

It is also difficult for ILL staffers to gain expertise on the numerous variety of databases available, most with unique search or ordering functions. While subject specialists might have expertise in a few databases, ILL/DDS staff processes requests that run the gamut of subjects. ILL/DDS staff seems to be more comfortable with full-text retrieval and document ordering from CD-ROM or leased databases that may be locally mounted or gatewayed through the library's OPAC, such as UnCover, UMI's ProQuest, or ADONIS. One problem here is that each commercial service must usually be searched one by one—none of the convenience of getting multiple holdings of hundreds of libraries in one "display holdings" command over OCLC, for example. Another is that most of the online document ordering from commercial suppliers is done over passworded systems. For security reasons, passwords and account numbers may only be supplied to a limited number of staff. If those individuals are absent, the order process is delayed.

Besides the online services, there are numerous other commercial services, some of which are very good, but which only have a printed or microfiche catalog of their inventory. While they may offer rapid delivery via fax, internal processing costs rise with each additional catalog that is checked and each additional step to enter an order in a non-standard way. (Even if the "nonstandard" order method is fast, such as telephone or fax, libraries that use an automated tracking system for statistical purposes may have to enter such requests manually into that system, whereas "regular" requests may be automatically downloaded from the OCLC or RLIN record.) If no commercial supplier lists the title and volume (preferably the specific article), or if the commercial supplier fails to fill the request, then the processing time was wasted because it is a rare article that is only available from commercial suppliers. There is no guarantee that the owning libraries will fulfill such requests either, but the odds improve as the list of potential library suppliers grows. Add the variety of databases available on research networks, electronic journals, and electronic listservs and bulletin boards, and ILL/DDS staff begin to feel like Alice in Wonderland. The electronic databases have increased the ability to verify difficult citations, but this too, must often be done on a catalog-by-catalog basis.

ILL staffers have experienced the frustration of trying to explain the "library of last resort concept" to a patron who has found a citation in the National Union Catalog and turns in a request with the comment, "It's available from the Library of Congress." Now, requests come in with "It's available from . . . " notes that span the world. If the citation is for a readily available trade publication or a fifteenth-century manuscript, the patron is positive that it really is available from the library which cited it online. After all, the Internet is a research network designed to foster resource sharing, is it not? ILL/DDS staffers listen daily to a litany of comments, such as, "The department's Subject Specialist told me that the library couldn't afford to buy this, but ILL would be able to get it for me. This library has it? How fast do you think you can get it? Could you call this library and let them know, I really need it bad! I don't think anyone else is likely to be doing research on, . . ."

Other examples of the need for ILL/DDS staff to require expertise include:

1. Vendors updates of software in use, requiring the purchase of new hardware or staff retraining, as when OCLC switched its ILL System to PRISM/PASSPORT software, and older OCLC workstations were no longer supported. Not only did the change affect OCLC-related products, but many libraries used other software, such as ILL request tracking systems, which also had to be upgraded or replaced in order to maintain OCLC compatibility.

2. Installation of new software, such as ARIEL from the Research Libraries Group, which allows articles to be scanned and transmitted over the Internet. Many libraries suffered installation problems, including IP addresses that did not work; interference with other software on the same workstation;

proper configuration of "extended memory" functions; not enough memory capacity (especially if hardware to meet minimum recommendations was acquired); incomplete transmissions, etc. Most libraries eventually worked out the problems, but not without extensive computer technical assistance.

3. Guidance in equipment purchases that are likely to require computer interfaces—expanded memory capacity for fax machines, for example.

4. Advice on multi-tasking capabilities of computer equipment, including determining the capacity or upgradeability of equipment on hand to handle additional functions versus acquiring dedicated workstations for specific functions. A small library processing under a thousand ILL requests per year might get by with one computer workstation for dialing into online bibliographic resources, using a modem with a fax board to convert the microcomputer to a fax machine for sending and retrieving documents via the Internet, and for e-mail. A large library might need one or more workstations for each function.

COPYRIGHT AND ILL/DDS

Another major issue with resource sharing as a means of alternative access is copyright compliance. While most publishers tend to believe that libraries constantly abuse the privilege of "fair use," copyright records almost invariably prove that libraries rarely send articles published within the last five years from the same journal more than the allowed five times within any calendar year. CONTU records have proven to be a valuable collection development selection tool. ILL records can prove whether the titles in which copyright guidelines were exceeded were likely to be a one-time occurrence (a single researcher working on a project for a limited time) or whether the pattern of use indicates a purchase may be needed. Subscription costs can be compared against the costs of alternative access, including both lending or delivery fees and copyright royalties. Even paying royalties on every document acquired from commercial suppliers can be cost effective when the delivery costs are reasonable and copyright royalties are not inflated beyond reason. Publishers could encourage further compliance, however, if they were to establish a flat fee for royalties so that libraries could budget for alternative access. Budgeting for royalty payments becomes a bigger economic factor as more libraries begin to rely on alternative access.

Fair use compliance in the United States usually follows the "rule of five." Laura Gasaway, a law librarian and noted authority on copyright issues in libraries, often points out that the "rule" is actually only a "suggestion." There are times when only one article or chapter is legitimately "fair use," as when a single patron wishes to copy an entire work or several articles from the same work. (If five different patrons get one article each, it is fair use; if one person wants five articles from within the same work, only one article is fair use.)

There are also times when more than five copies may be acquired and it is still fair use, as when a library subscribes to a journal, but a volume may be at the bindery or an article may have been ripped out so a replacement copy is required. (In such instances, more than five copies might be made as long as single copies are being made for various requesters.) Where the definition of fair use gets fuzzy is when resource sharing causes the cancellation of subscriptions or when a deliberate decision is made to rely on alternative access rather than to purchase a subscription. Both of these decisions are legitimate administrative options, and there are certainly times when alternative access is the right choice even when the pattern of use exceeds copyright guidelines. But as soon as a pattern of regular use is established and a decision "not to acquire" is made, then royalties are owed on every copy.

The issue becomes even trickier when a library enters into a resource sharing consortium for the purpose of canceling duplicate serial subscriptions among members of the consortium. It will probably take a ruling in a court of law to truly determine what is fair use and what is not in this instance. Publishers interpret current copyright guidelines as meaning that ANY subscription canceled under the provisions of a resource sharing agreement negates the fair use concept. Therefore, royalties are owed from copy one (or at the least, copy two) on every copy shared among consortium members. Libraries argue that seldom used serials would have to be canceled anyway due to budget limitations (usually caused by publishers' inflated institutional subscription costs), and as long as ILL/DDS records validate that less than six copies are acquired on an annual basis, normal CONTU guidelines apply. If the publisher's interpretation were to hold up in a court of law, then every bad selection decision ever made would haunt libraries through eternity, as would changes in the curriculum and missions of libraries and their governing boards. It is certainly a case of the tail wagging the dog when publishers tell libraries what they can and cannot buy or cancel. It is highly doubtful, however, that any library could build a defensible case if the pattern of use indicates fair use is exceeded on a regular basis year after year due to consortial resource sharing agreements, or even internally within a library system, as when branch libraries share the same materials rather than duplicating holdings. Paying royalties is a lot less expensive than defending one's library in court, so budgeting for royalty payments has to be an economic consideration in every resource sharing agreement.

Beyond the copyright/fair use issue, consortial resource sharing among libraries is not always the ideal solution to alternative access. Such arrangements work best when specific titles or subjects are agreed upon (keeping in mind the previous warning about fair use), such as expensive journals, monographic sets or microform sets likely to be used primarily by the holding library in the group. Each library still supports the primary needs of its own clientele, but might cancel subscriptions or avoid collecting in subject fields for which there is less demand, relying instead on the resources of another. Such arrangements work as long as all parties feel they are benefiting and no library is abused by the consortium. Coordination and close cooperation by all members is constantly required, and collection development decisions and deselection decisions can no longer be made independently among members of the consortium. It can work, and often does, with very strong relations developing among member libraries, but it does take effort. The hard part about such arrangements for ILL/DDS staffers is remembering (and sometimes even knowing about) which materials are included in specialized agreements. The borrowing library is likely to have to remember to add a note in the borrowing notes field to remind the lending library of the agreement, and every extra step in the process is one more chance for an error or delay.

RESOURCE SHARING AND ILL/DDS

Resource sharing agreements that are least likely to work are broad arrangements requiring priority service among members. Often, such arrangements are made outside the realm of ILL/DDS, with little knowledge of how many other such arrangements are already in effect or of the volume of trade between the libraries involved. Such arrangements look good on paper (particularly newspapers lauding the cooperative venture), and sound good when administrators are stating their case before the holders of the purse-strings. Unfortunately, the ILL/DDS units involved are not always given the equipment or the staff to actually provide priority service. Regular service with batch processing can be faster in the long-run than "priority" processes that require special handling. Any well-run ILL/DDS unit will have staff cross-trained to handle occasional staff absences, vacancies, and peak periods, but the first thing that gives when a unit is short-staffed is "priority or rush handling." Then the complaints start among consortia members, and formerly solid ILL/DDS relationships begin to deteriorate. Such arrangements should only be made on a very limited basis, with an extremely select group of libraries that are all committed and funded to meet the demands of the consortial agreement. If meeting consortial needs takes priority over other ILL/DDS operations, member libraries may even consider becoming nonsuppliers to other libraries, but before taking that drastic step, they must be very certain that the agreement will work.

Sometimes libraries involved are totally committed to a shared resources program and do provide the equipment and the staffing, possibly even instituting courier service and electronic transmission of documents between libraries. Even so, what looks good during the planning and implementation process may not be effective if the materials to be shared are in heavy demand within the home library. A recent experiment between the three state university libraries in Arizona found that the most common reason for unfilled requests among the three libraries was that the item was off the shelf or in circulation.

Service in one's own library may also be adversely affected by the demands from other libraries and users outside the library. If the ILL/DDS unit is constantly pulling current journals and popular books, then one's own patrons may be turning in "search" requests for materials that are frequently off the shelf. Most ILL/DDS units try to get materials reshelved as fast as possible, but a full-service unit may have a steady flow of requests for some titles. The lending unit may be responding to requests from other libraries; the document delivery unit may be responding to requests from branch campuses, or for items requested through an internal document delivery system. If the library has a fee-based service for nonregistered library users, that is another source of demand. No library wants to reach the point that the only way for its users to locate an item is to have the patron go through a document delivery service. If that is the case, closed stacks will make a comeback; U.S. libraries will once again want to consider a national periodical supply center; or, there will be more justification than ever for the virtual electronic library.

As libraries tighten their belts trying to stretch the materials budgets, fewer duplicate subscriptions and multiple copies of monographs are likely to be purchased. This puts more strain on access services staff processing requests for holds and searches. ILL receives more requests because copies are not on the shelves. Even though ILL codes no longer consider it an absolute "no-no" to acquire a title owned via ILL, the chances of filling a request for a popular title from another library may be just as difficult as acquiring a copy for use within one's own library. This is an area where nonmediated document delivery via commercial services can help. Patrons may have access to a variety of document delivery services where they can use a credit card to acquire journal articles. Some libraries have even set up accounts so that faculty and/or students can directly order materials while the library picks up the tab. While some people worry about the library's subsidizing the cost of delivery for journals owned, such use can be justified when frequently used items are often not available on the shelves. The impact of nonmediated document delivery on an ILL/DDS unit and other library staff requires setting up the accounts with various vendors, monitoring accounts, instructing users in how to be a do-it-yourself, and occasional troubleshooting. An advantage is that the end user absorbs more of the responsibility for follow-up and the cost of paper and toner and maintenance of heavily used fax equipment, though some libraries provide fax facilities or printers for this purpose.

While borrowing staff are trying to learn new search and retrieval techniques, lending staff are being retrained to electronically transmit materials to other libraries. Scanning techniques, while similar to photocopying, require retraining; this is also true when upgrading to fax equipment with delayed batch processes and computer interfaces. Switching to automated tracking of ILL records for copyright or statistical reporting requires retraining.

CONCLUSION

Electronic resource sharing has broadly expanded the duties and abilities of library staff and library users. Access to wide and diversified collections broadens the range of materials available to researchers today, which in turn affects the volume of interlibrary loan. Traditional ILL is more often combined with electronic document delivery from commercial suppliers. Keeping up with changing technology and the diversity of commercial document supply systems and products, as well as the multitude of resources available free on research networks, challenges ILL/DDS staff. Search and verification procedures are improving, but ordering is less systematic, requiring different techniques for numerous suppliers. ILL/DDS services are in the limelight, and expectations for rapid document delivery are high, but the level of service is not always quite up to the advertised productivity level of the suppliers. In an area where processes have long been noted as repetitive and tedious, staff are now swimming upstream trying not to drown in the swiftly changing currents of the document delivery field. The staff in the "leading edge" libraries are the first to face the

110

challenges and resolve technical problems. While it is doubtful that statutes will be raised in public places to honor these pioneering efforts, "bleeding edge" staff are to be commended for improving electronic resource sharing efforts in libraries around the world.

REFERENCES

1. Susan Hockey, "Developing Access to Electronic Texts in the Humanities," *Computers in Libraries* 13, no. 2 (1993) 41-43

2. Ruth M. Orenstein, ed., *BiblioData Fulltext Sources Online for Periodicals, Newspapers, Newsletters and Newswires*, vol 5, no. 1 (Needham Heights, MA: BiblioData, 1993).

3. Michael Strangelove, Diane Kovacs, and the Directory Team, Kent State University Libraries, *Directory of Electronic Journals, Newsletters and Academic Discussion Lists*, ed. Ann Okerson. 3d ed. (Washington, D.C.: Association of Research Libraries, 1993).

4. David L. Wilson, "Electronic Riches are Free on the Internet, but Some Worry About the Consequences," *Chronicle of Higher Education* 30, no. 47 (28 July 1993): A18, A20-21.

5. Dialog Information Services, *Full-text Sources: Alpha List* (Palo Alto, CA: 1992).

6. Wilson A20

7. Hockey 41-43.

8. Marilyn M. Roche, *ARL/RLG Interlibrary Loan Cost Study: A Joint Effort by the Association of Research libraries and the Research libraries Group.* (Washington, D.C.: Association of Research Libraries, 1993).

9 Eleanor Mitchell and Sheila Walters, *Document Delivery Services: Issues and Answers.* (Medford, NJ: Learned Informatin, 1995).

COST ANALYSIS FOR INTERLIBRARY LOAN:
A DIFFERENTIATED SERVICE

Amy Chang
Head of Access Services
Texas Tech University

INTRODUCTION

In 1992, the Association of Research Libraries and the Research Libraries Group conducted a joint project to analyze costs for Interlibrary Loan. The data included costs incurred by research libraries for both borrowing and lending units. Based on the survey of seventy-six research libraries, the final report of ARL/RLG ILL Cost Study was published in June, 1993. It appeared to be the first thorough cost study for ILL.

In the study report, the average cost was analyzed by numbers of cost categories, including ILL staff cost per transaction and unit cost. In addition, the mean and median costs were provided and the costs were categorized by the range of libraries. By adding its unit cost for borrowing to lending, the average cost for a complete ILL transaction was concluded to be $29.55. Because of budget constraints and the impact of commercial information services on document delivery, ILL becomes the first target for libraries to examine costs of obtaining material through the service. Since the study has been published, numerous local ILL cost analyses have followed. Many use the ARL average cost as a standard to determine the cost level of their ILL cost.

The ARL cost study reflects that ILL average cost per item is much higher than certain commercial offers. For instance, UnCover charges approximately $10.00 per article. In the process of evaluating ILL costs, it seems that libraries fail to take some other factors into account as they evaluate ILL costs.

This essay will identify the cost studies for ILL services, measure the quality service versus quantity service, view tangible sources and intangible ILL services from a user's perspective, and most important, differentiate ILL service from commercial document delivery.

COST STUDIES

The elements in the ARL//RLG ILL Cost Study include staffing, network and communications, document delivery, photocopying, supplies, equipment and software, rental and maintenance, and direct/indirect borrowing charges. These measurable and quantified factors are totaled and divided by the total number of filled requests for the average cost. The lending unit cost is conducted in the same manner. It shows that the average cost for per borrowing is $18.62 and for per lending is $10.92. A complete ILL transaction was concluded to be $29.55.

There are two ways to compute the ILL operational expenses, using the average

112

cost per item. For example, if the library borrows 10,000 borrowing items and supplies 8,000 lending items, this will cost the library $186,200 to borrow and $87,440 to lend. The actual total expenditure for ILL is $273,640.

	Total transactions	Average cost	Sub Total cost
Borrowing	10,000	$18.62	$186,200
Lending	8,000	$10.93	$ 87,440
Total	18,000	$29.55	$273,640

However, if we total the number of borrowing and lending and use the average cost $29.55 per item to compute the total expenditure, it would be $295,500 ($29.55 x 10,000 items). This would result in $21,860 extra toward the actual ILL expenditure and an additional $2.20 to per borrowing transaction. If the library lends more items than it borrows, the gap would be even larger. Only when the number of lending equals borrowing, the total cost of transaction of borrowing and lending, adding per item cost of lending to borrowing for a complete ILL transaction would this method not provide the actual expenditure figure.

To achieve cost-effectiveness, libraries should consider the "time/motion study." This study requires a primary time analysis for operational tasks involved in completing a request. For example, how much time is spent on searching the online database for each request, processing requests, packing, mailing, receiving materials, delivering materials, and filling requests. It converts the amount of time spent on a certain task into a dollar amount.

Since the work process must be broken down into small tasks, time/motion analyses enable the manager to identify time-consuming tasks in the work process. With this information, the manager will be able to focus on these tasks and to make alternatives for improvement.

A few differences between time/motion study and average cost study can be identified as follows:

* The "time/motion study" is based on the amount of time spent on each task, while the "average cost study" totals expenditures and averages the total number of filled requests.
* The time/motion study" counts each ILL request that is processed during a period of time. That means it may count a request more than once in various processes (e.g., the request is unable to be filled by the assigned libraries and needs to be reassigned and processed again). This particular request will get counted twice in the process request category. Also, if the unfilled request was searched, processed, and verified more than once before being found unattainable, it gets counted in each process. The "average cost study", however, averages the total cost by the total filled requests, considering one filled request as one count.

BORROWING COST VS. PURCHASING

The ILL cost can also be evaluated by the cost of purchasing. For example, in one fiscal year, the library borrows 2,000 unique book titles and 1,000 journal titles for 3,000 articles. Assuming the average cost of each journal title is $300, and $60 per book, these ILL materials would cost the library $420,000 to purchase. This amount does not include staffing, supplies, and any other processing costs to the library.

To borrow, however, costs $158,680 for these 2,000 books and 3,000 journal articles, using $29.55 average cost per ILL transaction. This total amount includes staffing, equipment, supplies, and telecommunications.

This is not to argue access vs. assets. Rather, this figure illustrates that the library can obtain research materials through ILL at a relatively reasonable cost, and research needs can be filled efficiently. Had money been available for purchase, the selection for purchasing new materials probably would not guarantee materials-on-demand.

QUALITY VS. QUANTITY

Unlike commercial information service, ILL is customized for a small community and not facilitated for filling quantity requests. The size of the community ILL serves could be from a few hundred to several thousand users. Through the services customized for users, Resource Sharing Network, and ILL librarian's expertise, libraries of all sizes are able to supply local users with a wide range of research sources.

In studying costs, one also needs to recognize the above elements of ILL in addition to quantified factors.

Customized Service

Materials loaned via ILL are not restricted to journals. Unlike commercial document delivery, ILL supplies current and out-of-print books, audio-visual materials, government documents, special collections, and microforms. Online databases and commercial delivery are utilized for various requests. Many libraries operate courier delivery service to deliver these materials among libraries or offer campus delivery to dormitories and faculty offices. At the same time, FAX and ARIEL are operated for transmitting articles and volumes of research materials that are shipped by US mail, UPS, and express mail. ILL staff utilize this range of delivery services to guarantee that materials are delivered to users quickly and are returned to the lenders safely.

Resource Sharing Networks

The electronic networks enable ILL to connect not only with libraries of all kinds but also with research institutes and commercial information services. This allows libraries to serve their users with rich research sources and also to globalize the access of the local library collections.

Additionally, the Internet has connected ILL librarians across the country. They help each other with verifications for obscured requests and communicate ILL policies. Via networks, knowledge of current technologies and new ideas are shared from coast to coast. Ultimately, this communication increases the quality of ILL service.

ILL Librarian

While bibliographic information is searched by a key stroke, and volumes of full text articles can be obtained online, to many researchers retrieving information from massive electronic databases is a haphazard effort. They still depend on ILL librarians' in-depth knowledge and skills of navigating databases and of using various reference tools. Most ILL librarians will exhaust all the sources in paper and electronic formats for an incomplete citation or foreign publication. Their expertise and connections are the key to making ILL a differentiated service.

INTANGIBLE VS. TANGIBLE

To many libraries, the goal is to add tangible materials to the library. Since ILL materials are loaned, not owned by the library, they are not considered to be tangibles to the library. Under this situation, ILL expense becomes a financial burden. This is probably why even when the increase of ILL is a fact of life to many libraries, equipment and staffing are not geared to sustain the growth.

Nevertheless, ILL materials are tangibles to users. Whether materials are loaned from another source or purchased for the local collection is transparent to users, so long as the library can supply the materials promptly. To satisfy the needs of users, the budget allocation for ILL must be planned, as if for acquiring materials for the local collection. The financial support must not be based merely on the quantitative growth of the service, but on the development of quality service.

CONCLUSION

The ILL cost study must be used as a tool to discern the strengths and weaknesses of the local ILL service. This information will allow the library to customize service for users, use resources in a cost effective manner to maximize access through resource-sharing networks, and to develop a more sophisticated delivery system.

Despite the fact that volumes of articles are increasingly accessible electronically, the need for ILL continues to grow nationwide. The OCLC Resource Sharing Report shows that there were 6.8 million ILL transactions on OCLC in 1994. These data only reflect 23% of the entire ILL market, which indicates that the need for person-to-person ILL service still remains strong.

As more research materials are digitized, more users will access research information electronically at their own workstation. Inevitably, new technology will alter ILL and document delivery once again. To survive in today's ever-changing world, ILL must be evaluated and reevaluated on an ongoing basis in order to allow new and unique services to be strategically developed for information users. To guarantee a role in tomorrow's information market, libraries must envision new ways to fulfill the demands of information users.

115

INTERLIBRARY LOAN:
A COOPERATIVE EFFORT AMONG OCLC USERS

Kate Nevins
Executive Director
SOLINET

Darryl Lang
Former Manager of
Market Research & Analysis
OCLC

INTRODUCTION

OCLC introduced its Interlibrary Loan (ILL) System in 1979. Since that time, each year has brought significant growth in the number of libraries using the system and the amount of activity they generate. Our analysis of a five-year period shows continued increase as well as cooperation among libraries of all types across a wide geographical area.

Many libraries direct their borrowing efforts toward local and regional resources, as specified in the National Interlibrary Loan Code and in many state and local codes. Despite this extensive use of local resources, our analysis shows that no geographic area or type of library group is entirely self sufficient in meeting its ILL needs.

This essay presents patterns of ILL activity in the United States based on use of the OCLC ILL System. As a result, the information does not reflect ILL activity conducted through other means. Unfortunately, no single source consolidates information about ILL activity nationwide.

The role of the OCLC ILL System varies widely from library to library. Some use it as a primary source, while others use it only as a last resort. Knowledge about specific local and regional practices will provide an important perspective on this data for libraries wanting to analyze their own usage.

These findings result from an analysis of transactions from the OCLC ILL System from fiscal 1986 to fiscal 1991. OCLC's fiscal year extends from July 1 to June 30. The OCLC ILL System tracks each request initiated by a borrowing library, or received by a lending library. In counting the number of libraries using the system, we have defined borrowing libraries as those that initiated at least one borrowing request and lending libraries as those that lent at least one item during the period.

GROWTH IN BORROWING AND LENDING ON THE OCLC ILL SYSTEM

The demand for materials via the OCLC ILL System escalated dramatically during the five-year period ending with fiscal 1991; borrowing requests doubled to 5.4 million from 2.7 million in fiscal 1986. At the same time, the number of items lent rose to 4.5 million from 2.3 million in fiscal 1986, an increase of 98 percent.

Even with this rapid growth, the percentage of borrowing requests that were eventually filled remained steady at about 86 percent. (Note: This percentage was calculated by dividing the number of items borrowed by the number of borrowing requests. We counted a request as filled when the library initiating the request borrowed the requested item.)

The number of libraries using the OCLC ILL System also increased substantially during this period, but at a slower pace than the number of borrowing requests and items lent. In addition, the growth rate in the number of libraries was higher for borrowing than for lending. The number of libraries requesting items increased from 3,019 in fiscal 1986 to 4,643 in fiscal 1991, a 54 percent rise. The number of libraries that lent materials increased at a slower rate, 37 percent, from 2,884 in fiscal 1986 to 3,958 in fiscal 1991.

From these Figures, we can attribute the bulk of growth to individual libraries increasing their use of the OCLC ILL System rather than to additional libraries beginning to use the system. The average number of borrowing requests per library rose by 30 percent, from 896 per library in fiscal 1986 to 1,165 in fiscal 1991. The average number of items lent per library grew at the higher rate of 44 percent, from 786 in fiscal 1986 to 1,134 in fiscal 1991.

Nearly two million items were provided as photocopies on the OCLC ILL System during fiscal 1991. This Figure represents 44 percent of total items lent in fiscal 1991, one that hardly changed from the 41 percent photocopy provision rate for fiscal 1986. (Note: The number of photocopies was not available directly from ILL data transactions. Instead, we assumed that an item was provided as a photocopy when the lending library did not specify a due date for returning it.)

Borrowing and Lending Libraries (Fy90-91)
By Type

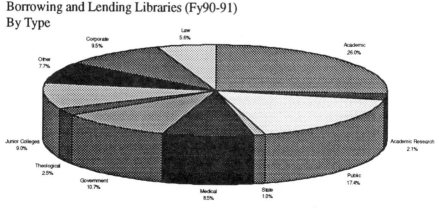

Fig. 12.1a Number of Borrowing Libraries

117

Borrowing and Lending Libraries (Fy90-91)
By Type

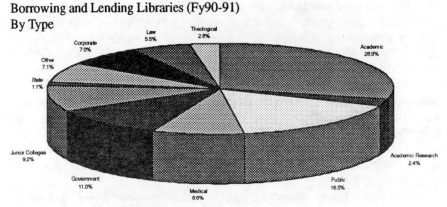

Fig. 12.1b Number of Lending Libraries

BORROWING AND LENDING BY TYPE OF LIBRARY

Among library types, academic libraries, defined as those connected with four-year colleges and universities and including specialized academic libraries (e.g., medical, law, and theological), ranked first in total borrowing and lending volume on the OCLC ILL System during fiscal 1991, as shown in Fig 12.1a and Fig 12.1b Public libraries ranked second in total borrowing activity, while academic research libraries (defined as those belonging to the Association of Research Libraries) were second in total lending activity.

Academic libraries also led in the number of borrowing and lending libraries for fiscal 1991, followed by public libraries in both activity categories, as Fig 12.2a and Fig 12.2b shows. The rankings of these library types in volume and number of libraries were the same in fiscal 1991 as they had been in fiscal 1986.

Academic research libraries were by far the most active individual users of the OCLC ILL System, having the highest average number of total items borrowed and

Table 12.1. OCLC Definitions of Library Type Categories

LIBRARY TYPE	DEFINITIONS
ACADEMIC	LIBRARIES FROM FOUR YEAR UNIVERSITIES OR COLLEGES, INCLUDING MAIN AND AUXILIARY CAMPUS LIBRARIES AND SPECIALIZED ACADEMIC LIBRARIES, SUCH AS MEDICAL, LAW, AND THEOLOGICAL
ACADEMIC RESEARCH	ACADEMIC LIBRARIES THAT BELONG TO THE ASSOCIATION OF RESEARCH LIBRARIES
CORPORATE	LIBRARIES SERVING CORPORATIONS, EXCLUDING LAW FIRMS AND MEDICAL ORGANIZATIONS
GOVERNMENT	LOCAL AND FEDERAL LIBRARIES, INCLUDING SPECIALIZED GOVERNMENT LIBRARIES, SUCH AS LAW AND MEDICAL
JUNIOR COLLEGE	LIBRARIES SERVING TWO-YEAR COLLEGES
LAW	LIBRARIES SERVING LAW FIRMS, LAW SCHOOLS, AND LOCAL, STATE AND FEDERAL COURTS
MEDICAL	LIBRARIES SERVING MEDICAL SCHOOLS, HOSPITALS, MEDICAL RESEARCH ORGANIZATIONS, AND COUNTRY AND STATE HEALTH AGENCIES
PUBLIC	PUBLIC LIBRARIES AND THEIR BRANCHES, PUBLIC LIBRARY SYSTEMS, AND REGIONAL LIBRARIES
STATE	LIBRARIES SERVING AS A STATE LIBRARY AGENCY FOR AN INDIVIDUAL STATE
THEOLOGICAL	LIBRARIES SERVING CHURCHES, SEMINARIES, AND OTHER RELIGIOUS ORGANIZATIONS
OTHER TYPES	LIBRARIES NOT INCLUDED IN OTHER CATEGORIES, SUCH AS MUSEUMS, ASSOCIATIONS, PROCESSING CENTERS, SCHOOLS, AND INSTITUTES

Borrowing and Lending Volume (Fy90-091)
By Type

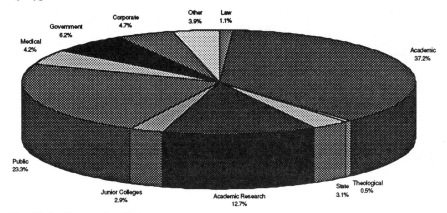

Fig. 12.2a Borrowing Volume

Borrowing and Lending Volume (Fy90-90)
By Type

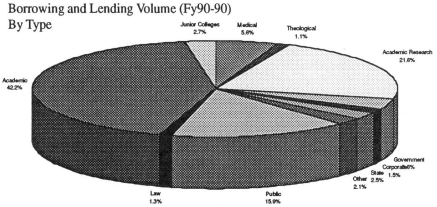

Fig. 12.2b Lending Volume

lent per library during fiscal 1991, as shown in Table 12.2. This group consisted of a relatively small number of libraries that generated a large volume in borrowing and lending activity.

Borrowing and lending often occurred between different library types, though the highest percentage usually took place between libraries in the same category, ranging from about a third to half of all items borrowed or lent. Table 12.3 shows major borrowing activity between library types during fiscal 1991 for academic, public, and academic research libraries. Each group borrowed most frequently from libraries of the same type. Table 12.4 shows comparable Figures for lending activity. Academic and public libraries lent most often to other libraries in the same category, while academic research libraries lent more often to academic libraries than to other

Table 12.2. Average Number of Borrows and Loans Per Library Type (FY90-91). Sorted by average number of borrows.

	FY90-91 AVERAGE # OF BORROWS PER LIBRARY	FY90-91 AVERAGE # OF LOANS PER LIBRARY
ACADEMIC RESEARCH	6,300	10,532
STATE	3,073	2,522
ACADEMIC	1,485	1,680
PUBLIC	1,391	1,109
GOVERNMENT	603	375
OTHER TYPES	523	339
MEDICAL	514	751
CORPORATE	511	249
JUNIOR COLLEGES	336	332
THEOLOGICAL	214	436
LAW	211	262

Table 12.3. Borrowing Between Library Types (FY 91).

BORROWER	LENDER	% OF ITEMS
ACADEMIC (TOTAL ITEMS 1,737,192)	ACADEMIC	55.2
	ACADEMIC RESEARCH	23
	PUBLIC	5.9
	MEDICAL	4.8
	SUBTOTAL	88.9
PUBLIC (TOTAL ITEMS 1,08,681)	PUBLIC	42.1
	ACADEMIC	31.9
	ACADEMIC RESEARCH	10.7
	STATE	5.5
	SUBTOTAL	90.2
ACADEMIC RESEARCH (TOTAL ITEMS 592,163)	ACADEMIC RESEARCH	45
	ACADEMIC	36.3
	MEDICAL	5
	PUBLIC	4.7
	SUBTOTAL	91

academic research libraries. Tables 12.3 and 12.4 reveal fairly extensive interaction between academic and public libraries, as well as between academic and academic research libraries.

BORROWING AND LENDING BY STATE

Four states accounted for more than a quarter of all borrowing and lending activity during fiscal 1991. California, Texas, New York, and Pennsylvania ranked highest in borrowing volume, accounting for a combined 26.9 percent of all items borrowed. These states also led in lending activity, accounting for 28.5 percent of all items lent.

Table 12.4. Lending Between Library Types (FY 91).

LENDER	BORROWER	% OF ITEMS
ACADEMIC	ACADEMIC	49.2
(TOTAL ITEMS 1,894,737)	PUBLIC	17.3
	ACADEMIC RESEARCH	11
	CORPORATE	3.9
	SUBTOTAL	81.4
ACADEMIC RESEARCH	ACADEMIC	40.5
(TOTAL ITEMS 968,917)	ACADEMIC RESEARCH	26.7
	PUBLIC	11.4
	CORPORATE	5.7
	SUBTOTAL	84.3
PUBLIC	PUBLIC	59.5
(TOTAL ITEMS 714,490)	ACADEMIC	13.9
	STATE	6.9
	ACADEMIC RESEARCH	3.7
	SUBTOTAL	84

Of these four states, all but Texas also ranked among the top four in the number of borrowing and lending libraries. Texas ranked ninth in borrowing and sixth in lending. As a result, Texas had a higher average number of items borrowed and lent per library than did the other three states.

Table 12.4 also shows how much of each state's borrowing and lending occurred among libraries within the state. For example, 82.2 percent of all items borrowed by California libraries in fiscal 1991 came from other libraries in California, representing the highest proportion of in-state borrowing. New Jersey led in the proportion of in-state lending, since 84.2 percent of items lent by New Jersey libraries went to other libraries in the state. Overall, 63 percent of all fiscal 1991 activity occurred among libraries in the same state. No state relied solely on libraries within the state for borrowing or lending.

For any state, the amount of in-state activity conducted via the OCLC ILL System depended on its size and location as well as the predominant ILL method employed in that state.

CONCLUSIONS

Trends indicate that the growth of ILL volume via the OCLC ILL System will continue. In the face of this growth, three important issues emerge. We believe that libraries and OCLC should:

1. Maintain ILL tools that support ILL traffic on a wide geographic basis and across library types;
2. Improve the efficiency of the OCLC ILL System through enhancements and features to help libraries cope with increased ILL activity and limited staff resources; and

3.   Accommodate the ILL requirements of high-volume lenders to ensure the availability of their resources.

OCLC and member libraries are committed to the ILL process. The OCLC ILL System is an important tool that helps libraries expand the availability of resources for their patrons.

The chapter is a condensed reprint from the the Wilson Library Bulletin, February, 1993 p.37-40, 110. Editors would like to thank the Wilson Library Bulletin for granting permission.

At the time this essay was written Darryl Lang was a Manager of Market Research & Analysis for OCLC.

Index

ABI/Info 44
Access Colorado Library Information
Network 20
ACLIN See Access Colorado Library
Information Network
ADONIS 4, 11, 18, 20, 29, 33, 35,
36, 38, 45, 99, 105
American Chemical Society 45
American Library Association 62, 77
American Mathematical Society 29, 36
ARIEL 21, 22, 28, 38, 44, 46, 56,
75, 78, 79, 85, 94, 95, 106,
114
Arizona State University 18, 97
ARL See Association of Research
Libraries
ARL/RLG 11, 76, 82, 88, 90, 96,
102, 104, 111, 112
ARTel 27
Article Express 11, 29, 33, 34, 35,
38
ASCII 20, 100
Association of Research Libraries 5,
11, 12, 13, 15, 16, 23, 24,
29, 30, 42, 76, 77, 78, 82,
83, 84, 88, 90, 95, 96, 102,
104, 111, 112, 118
ASU See Arizona State University
AVISO 64, 65, 67, 70, 71, 72, 73,
74, 75, 78, 95

BiblioData 31, 98, 111
BLDSC See British Library Document
Supply Centre
British Library Document Supply
Centre 18, 27, 28, 33, 34, 35,
44
Bryn Mawr College 99

CAN/DOC 27
CAN/OLE See Canadian National
Union Catalog Online Enquiry

Canada Institute for Scientific and
Technical Info 27, 70
Canadian National Union Catalog
Online Enquiry 26, 27
CARL See Colorado Alliance of
Research Libraries
CAS See Chemical Abstracts Service
CASIAS See Current Awareness
Service Individual Article Service
Chemical Abstracts Service 33, 34,
36, 40, 45, 53
CIC See Committee on Institutional
Cooperation
CitaDel 18, 44, 50, 104
Clearinghouse for Networked Informa-
tion Discovery 99
Cleveland, Gary 19
Colorado Alliance of Research
Libraries 20, 24, 44
Colorado State University 17, 18
Committee on Institutional Coopera-
tion 78, 84, 85
CONTU 107, 108
Copyright 6, 7, 8, 9, 12, 17, 18, 20,
22, 28, 30, 32, 41, 45, 49, 56
64, 68, 75, 78, 98, 99, 104,
105, 107, 108, 110
Cost Study 5, 11, 76, 82, 85, 88,
90, 96, 102, 104, 111, 112,
113, 115
Council of Library Resource 43
Current Awareness Service Individual
Article Service 18

Dartmouth College 99
DIALOG 27, 29, 34, 35, 36, 45, 53
99, 105, 111
Dynamic Information 28, 33, 36,
38, 39

Engineering Society Library 27

fee-based 18, 22, 28, 50, 109
file transfer protocols 20, 21, 30, 99
FirstSearch 15, 18, 36, 45, 50, 53
FIZ Karlsruhe 34
FoxPro 65, 74, 75
FTP *See* file transfer protocols

Gasaway, Laura 107
Genuine Article 11, 29, 33
Gillespie, P. D. 26, 31

IAC *See* Information Access Corporation
ILL Cost Study 82, 112, 115
Information Access Corporation 18, 20, 46, 78
Institute for Scientific Information 18, 29, 33, 39, 40
International Standardization Organization 14, 72
ISI *See* Institute for Scientific Information
ISM *See* Library Information Systems of Toronto Canada
ISO *See* International Standardization Organization
ISO ILL Protocol 75

Japan Information Center of Science and Technology 34

LAN *See* local area networks
Library Information Systems of Toronto Canada 65, 70, 71, 72, 75
local area networks 16, 17, 23, 65, 78, 98, 100

MathDoc 29, 33, 36
MELVYL 16
MIME *See* Multipurpose Internet Mail Extension
Multipurpose Internet Mail Extension 21, 22

NAILDD *See* North American Interlibrary Loan/Document Delivery
National Library of Canada 27, 71, 72
National Library of Medicine 15, 45
National Union Catalog 26, 106
NCSU *See* North Carolina State University
NLM *See* National Library of Medicine
North American Interlibrary Loan/Document Delivery 16, 24, 75
North Carolina State University 20, 46
Northwestern University 82

OCLC 4, 5, 6, 11, 12, 14, 15, 16, 17, 18, 20, 24, 27, 34, 36, 44, 45, 56, 60, 65, 70, 71, 75, 78, 79, 80, 81, 88, 89, 90, 91, 93, 94, 95, 104, 105, 106, 115, 116, 117, 118, 121, 122
OCLC ILL 15, 17, 27, 90, 116, 117, 118, 121
Ohio State University 20, 46, 84
Okerson, Ann 29, 111
OPAC 13, 17, 23, 65, 71, 79, 98, 99, 100, 105

PRISM 15, 18, 78, 79, 106
ProQuest 5, 20, 45, 99, 105

Research Libraries Group 5, 11, 18, 21, 38, 44, 46, 50, 53, 76, 78, 82, 85, 88, 90, 94, 96, 102, 104, 111, 112
Research Libraries Information Network 14, 15, 27, 34, 50, 71, 75, 78, 80, 81, 98, 105, 106
RLG *See* Research Libraries Group
RLIN *See* Research Libraries Information Network

124

ROMULUS 27, 70, 71

Syracuse University 43, 47
Systems Development Corp 26

TELNET 17, 71, 98
Texas Tech University 52, 95, 112
Total Quality Management 52, 53,
    54, 55, 57, 58, 59, 61, 62,
    86, 88, 95, 96
TQM *See* Total Quality Management
Triangle Research Libraries Net-
    work 8, 9
TRLN *See* Triangle Research Librar-
    ies Network
TYMNET 34

UC *See* University of Colorado
UCLA 6
UMI 5, 18, 20, 28, 33, 34, 35,
    38, 39, 40, 44, 45, 99, 105
UNC-CH *See* University of North
    Carolina-Chapel Hill
UnCover 5, 11, 17, 18, 20, 29,
    33, 35, 38, 39, 44, 53, 65,
    99, 105, 112
University of California 12, 16, 24
University of Colorado 13, 17. 18,
    24
University of Houston 86
University of North Carolina-Chapel
    Hill 9
University of Texas 40

Washington Library Network 15
WLN 15
World Wide Web 21

Z39.5 70, 71, 100